Self-Healing
with the
NADI TECHNIQUE

THE
HOLISTIC
WAY

About the Author

BILLY ROBERTS lives in picturesque Cornwall (southwest England) with his wife, Dolly, and their two pussycats, Elly and Poppy. For many years he was a member of the National Federation of Spiritual Healers, but today he works independently of any organization. He founded the Thought Workshop, the UK's first center for psychic and spiritual studies and alternative therapies, which later became the Billy Roberts Paranormal Study Centre, visited by esoteric students from all over the world.

Billy lectures and conducts workshops on a wide range of healing practices and is the author of twenty-five books, including *The Healing Paw* (Harper Collins) and *So You Want To Be Psychic* (John Hunt Publishing). He has appeared on television worldwide and has presented his own thirty-six-week television series, *Secrets of the Paranormal*. In 2003 he was featured in a documentary to promote Sony's PlayStation 2 game Ghost Hunter, filmed on location in New Orleans and the Gulf of Mexico. He also made several appearances on the popular television series *Most Haunted* and has more recently finished filming the pilot to a new television series, *Living with Angels and Demons*.

Self-Healing
with the
NADI TECHNIQUE

THE
HOLISTIC
WAY

BILLY ROBERTS

Llewellyn Publications
WOODBURY, MINNESOTA

FIRST EDITION
First Printing, 2013

Cover design by Lisa Novak
Cover's abstract holiday background by iStockphoto.com/Anna Omelchenko and transcending design by iStockphoto.com/stereohype
Interior illustrations by Llewellyn Art Department

Llewellyn Publications is a registered trademark
of Llewellyn Worldwide Ltd.

Library of Congress Cataloging-in-Publication Data
Roberts, Billy, 1946–
 The holistic way : self-healing with the nadi technique / Billy Roberts.
—First edition.
    pages   cm
 Includes bibliographical references and index.
 ISBN 978-0-7387-3610-5
1. Breathing exercises—Therapeutic use. 2. Health. 3. Mind and body. I. Title.
 RA782.R63 2013
 613′.192—dc23
                                                      2013007927

Llewellyn Publications
A Division of Llewellyn Worldwide Ltd.
2143 Wooddale Drive
Woodbury, MN 55125-2989
www.llewellyn.com

Printed in the United States of America

Contents

Nadi Techniques

Figures

Introduction

In this health-conscious age of science and technology, more and more people are moving away from the more conventional allopathic medicine in an effort to find alternative ways of treating their ailments. It is now the general consensus of opinion that many of the so-called modern medicines prescribed by our physicians often produce side effects, and although they do directly treat the condition, the long-term effects of many prescribed drugs are really unknown, even though they are subjected to many years of testing. Perhaps to the pharmaceutical companies the cure far outweighs the side effects, and the damage (albeit minor in many cases) caused by many prescribed medicines is a small price to pay.

I am speaking as someone who has spent my entire life on antibiotics and other drugs in the treatment of an incurable and, at times, debilitating respiratory disease that I contracted when I was three years old. I must say that I would not have survived at all had it not been for antibiotics, inhalers, and other medications that treated infections and stabilized my condition. As a child in the 1950s I had no choice, and like all sickly children simply had to smile and take the medicine.

Because of my health condition, I took an avid interest in medicine and read as many medical books and journals as I could in an effort to understand my health problem and how drugs affected the other components that make up my body.

In fact, my interest in alternative or complementary medicine started around the age of thirteen. It was an interest I inherited from my mother, who lovingly took me as a young child to faith healers, herbalists, homeopaths, and many other alternative practitioners in an effort to rid me of this awful disease, bilateral basal bronchiectasis, which necessitated long periods in the hospital and physiotherapy every day to keep my lungs clear of mucus. My mother believed wholeheartedly in such treatments, and even though many of the treatments were quite bizarre and a waste of time, she never lost heart and continued relentlessly in her search for a cure.

Vegetarianism and Health

I became a vegetarian when I was fourteen, partly because of my inherent love of animals but also because I had read much about the way our diet has a profound effect on our health. In fact, after the first six months of not eating meat or consuming any dairy products at all, I noticed a vast improvement in my breathing. I was also producing less sputum, one of the many causes of ongoing infections. While a vegetarian diet does not suit everybody, particularly people who suffer with anemia or require high-protein diets, by the time I was fifteen my hospital physician was so pleased with my improvement that my monthly hospital appointments were changed to biannual visits.

A nutritionally well-balanced diet is not only essential to keep the physical body healthy and in good working order, but it is also important in the assimilation of prana, or energy, and to maintain the efficiency of the subtle energy system. Winnie Lord (now deceased), the dietitian at the Thought Workshop, my center in

Liverpool, England, explained to me that the color of the food we eat is equally as important as the nutritional content, and that we should always appreciate and mentally absorb the color value of what we are eating. She also said that when children are taught this from a very early age, it encourages harmony and balance, essential for psychological as well as physical growth. It was Winnie Lord who inspired me to include energy food and its nutritional properties in the nadi technique.

The nadi technique is an effective method of maintaining balance and harmony in the energetic system, with the sole intention of improving the overall health of the body. Over the years it has helped me immensely to cope with bronchiectasis, an incurable lung disease I contracted when I was three. Apart from this, though, the nadi technique has helped me to be much more mentally focused, and it has taught me to be more aware and to know my own body.

Music, the Sixties, and Drugs

Although I wasn't supposed to live to see my teens, I did, and when I left school in 1962 at the age of sixteen, my life had taken on an even greater surprise to everyone who knew me: I had been playing the guitar since I was nine years old, and all of a sudden I was living the dream of every other kid my age by playing lead guitar in a rock band. Throughout the 1960s I toured Europe with my band, the Kruzads, supporting such musical giants as Chuck Berry, the Moody Blues, Memphis Slim, the Yardbirds, and Jimi Hendrix, to name but a few. This was a magical age when love, peace, and Transcendental Meditation became the mantra of my generation. Although in the 1960s music was all that I wanted to do, I was still very much aware of the spiritual side of my life and knew that my spiritual energies had been channeled into the creative areas of my life. Spiritual energy more often than not encourages the development of creative skills, such as the propensity toward music or any artistic tendency. Even in my musical years I still felt as though I was being influenced by some immense, powerful spiritual force and that my career as a rock musician was merely preparation for something much more meaningful, spiritually speaking.

Although you would be forgiven for wondering what all this has to do with this book, it is an integral part of my personal healing process and the very reason why I was led to the creation of the nadi technique, a holistic healing system I have now used successfully for over thirty years.

As a result of living life in the proverbial fast lane and the excesses of my profession as a musician, I became addicted to a wide range of narcotic substances; by 1970, extremely ill, I was forced to return to the UK to be cared for by my mother. The impact of this on my childhood illness was catastrophic, and I found myself fighting two battles: one of drug addiction and the other my lung condition, which had now returned with a vengeance.

Needless to say, it was at the lowest point in my life that some incredibly powerful spiritual force took control of my destiny and gradually turned things around completely. Although most of this was, in fact, self-created, it was clear to me that I had to do something to help myself. I had exhausted all avenues—clinics, psychiatric counseling, and psychological therapies of all sorts—and although I had completely freed myself from my addictions, the emotional aftermath was even worse. My years of drug abuse had shattered my confidence and self-esteem. I'd lost my career as a musician and found myself alone and depressed. I had developed an anxiety neurosis to the extreme: I was claustrophobic and agoraphobic. I was living in a veritable hell and knew that I simply could not go on this way.

I had studied and practiced meditation in the sixties and had once met the Maharishi Mahesh Yogi, the innovator of Transcendental Meditation, or TM, as it is referred to. I practiced it religiously, without success. It just did not work for me in the way I so badly needed. It was at that point I began to experiment with various systems of meditation and visualization techniques and finally created a method that suited me perfectly.

Buddhism and Yoga

Although I had been brought up as a Christian, like many people in the so-called Flower Power period of the sixties, I had been very interested in Buddhism and now found its underlying philosophy a great help when I needed it most. I took up hatha yoga and began to make a detailed study of it as a psychological tool to help me in my struggle to gain control and establish some normality in my life. Although I didn't quite know it then, this was the first step to creating a system of healing and self-improvement that I would use only a few years later.

I read everything I could on self-improvement techniques, healing methods, yogic philosophy, and numerous psychology books. Although I have only ever read his books, I have always regarded Yogi Ramacharaka as my first (absent) spiritual mentor, as it was his *Fourteen Lessons in Yogi Philosophy and Oriental Occultism* that set me firmly on what yogi masters refer to as the Path of Attainment, my guiding light even today.

Spiritual Healing

I always regard the early 1970s as my period of study and preparation, as it was during the 1970s that I seriously looked at formulating some sort of healing system that was different.

In 1979, after serving a two-year period (this is the required amount of time in the UK) as a trainee healer under the supervision of various healers in Spiritualist churches and centers, I became a fully fledged member of the National Federation of Spiritual Healers (NFSH) and received my certificate allowing me to practice under the auspices of the largest healing organization in the UK. I then went on the register of the NFSH, which referred people to me for healing.

It was during this time that I noticed many people who consulted me were often more in need of some sort of reassurance and counseling rather than healing. Although I had every faith in my own abilities as a healer, the last thing I wanted to do was fill someone who was dying with false hope. In fact, I found it quite upsetting, and for a time questioned whether or not I should be doing it at all. At the time, apart from the more traditional spiritual healing, I also was studying the effects of magnetic and pranic healing. While spiritual healing calls upon a higher spiritual power to heal, magnetic and pranic healing encourage the body to normalize and heal itself.

1980: The Beginning

Primarily because of my Aunt Louise's enthusiastic encouragement and influence, I began working professionally as a medium on the Spiritualist circuit. Aunt Louise was a well-known British medium during the 1940s and '50s, and it was she who took me under her wing, so to speak, and pointed me in the right direction, at least where my mediumship was concerned. Because of my radical approach to mediumship, I attracted a following and was soon invited to work all over the UK and then overseas.

My style of mediumship appealed more to the younger members of the audience as opposed to the older diehard Spiritualists who, for reasons best known to themselves, regarded the way I demonstrated my mediumistic skills as more suited to the public arena of a theater rather than a religious environment. I always felt, sometimes to my own detriment, that the way mediumship was presented needed modernizing in order to attract a younger audience. This I did with some success.

With healing, there is always the danger of becoming delusional and thinking that you are something you are not, and so I had to stand back and assess my potential and really look at what I wanted to do and what I was endeavoring to achieve. Because of all I had been through, introspective analysis (as Jung termed it) was difficult but necessary before I embarked upon something that was in great danger of ridicule. After all, I was now known for my mediumistic skills more than I was for my healing abilities. Would a new healing system be accepted—or rejected? By this time, there were many shiatsu, reflexology, and Touch for Health (TFH) therapists around, and the last thing I needed was to be seen as producing a therapy that was contrary to anything any of these offered.

The Thought Workshop

By 1982 I had seriously begun to create a system that involved various types of healing, but which I hoped transcended the parameters of other traditional therapies and treated the whole person as opposed to just the affected part. I needed a base from which to work, as well as people who were qualified in various types of therapies to work with. It was at that point I created the Thought Workshop, the north of England's very first center for psychic and spiritual studies and alternative therapies.

The more popular the Thought Workshop became, the more I realized that I needed more knowledge about the craft I was endeavoring to use. I studied metaphysical and transcendental healing at the Metaphysical Research Center in London, which helped me gain more knowledge about energy transference and how it could affect the healing process. I had always been fascinated with the teachings of the Rosicrucian Society and their approach to metaphysics, and so I joined AMORC in an attempt to learn more and broaden my horizons. It was around this time that I also became involved with the Greater World Christian Spiritualist Association, based in Holland Park, London. I eventually became a certified healer with them.

As far as I was concerned, the Thought Workshop had done its job as far as it could, and so in the mid-90s I closed it down and established the Billy Roberts Paranormal Study Centre on the famous Penny Lane of Beatles fame, visited by students from all over the world. I disbanded this in 2006 primarily to allow me the time to take my workshops all over the UK and to other countries.

The Nadi Technique Defined

In esoteric parlance, *prana* is the term used to describe all energy in the universe; it is essential for the maintenance of the health and ultimately for the life of the physical body. It is drawn in with each breath and may be controlled through the process of rhythmic breathing. It is one of the functions of the major chakras to modify and distribute the inflowing prana to the organs of the body, encouraging balance and harmony on all levels. Although the word *nadi* literally means "nerve" only at a more subtle level, nadis are, in fact, integral parts of a network of minute channels that permeate the subtle anatomy, the replicated and more refined spiritual part of our being. To all intents and purposes, nadis look like veins, but instead of conveying blood they support the major channels, meridians, in the relentless process of transporting prana throughout the subtle and physical bodies, ensuring their health and efficiency.

In yoga, nadis are equated with the branches of a tree, and the meridians, the more major channels, with the trunk of the tree. Although the nadis are considered to be the minor channels, they are vitally important in the whole process of maintaining levels of energy in the subtle anatomy. Gradually I discovered that by controlling and manipulating energy through the nadis, inner balance could be maintained and the overall health of the body improved.

And so I began to seriously create what I call the nadi technique, a system of holistic healing that works for me and helps me to achieve a healthier life as well as restore some semblance of order to my mind. As a healing system, the nadi technique is fairly eclectic, combining all the different skills I have developed over the years to form one holistic treatment. As far as I was concerned, the system was extremely simple yet very effective. It worked on me and also produced excellent positive results when I applied it to other people.

The word *holistic* simply means "the whole" as opposed to the part. Although one single application from the nadi technique may easily be effectively used to treat a particular condition, it is more effective when applied to the whole person. I work on the age-old premise as posed by Paracelsus (a German/Swiss physician and alchemist, 1493–1541): that all health conditions have

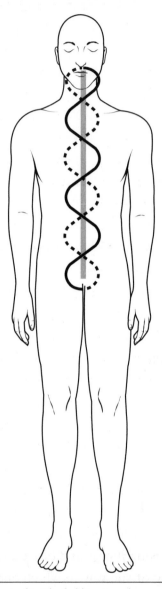

FIGURE 1: *Main nadis. Shaded line is sushumna, or spinal nadi. Solid line is ida (feminine) nadi, which begins in the left nostril and controls the right side of the body. Dotted line is pingala (masculine) nadi, which begins in the right nostril and controls the left side of the body.*

some origins in the mind. Paracelsus believed that the mind is the common denominator and is the grand emperor over its kingdom—the body and its individual components that make up the whole. It can either put you into an early grave or improve your health and longevity. Although I began using the nadi technique at the Thought Workshop in the mid-1980s, it was then in its innovative stages and not as fully formed as it is today.

The nadi technique is an effective holistic system designed to promote a healthier body, mind, and spirit by encouraging the movement of energy through the intricate network of nadis and meridians. It is as effective on yourself as it is on someone else, and it involves the processes of touch, thought, and feeling. It can be administered either in close proximity or at a great distance with the use of thought techniques; the results are nearly always the same.

The system is much more than a series of exercises to heal and expand the awareness; it also contains a core of teachings to encourage a deeper understanding of the universe and the law of attraction. The nadi technique consists of simple exercises to encourage a more even and consistent flow of energy through the nadis that permeate the body. In fact, complementary practitioners perceive good health as being the result of an unrestricted flow of energy, and disease and poor health as a restriction of the movement of energy in one or more of the delicate channels. This restriction produces a corresponding effect on the organs of the physical body, thus causing illness and disease to become apparent. An understanding of the way in which energy is processed through the nadis and the subtle anatomy will help you gain greater control of the way your body and mind function, which will improve the overall quality of your life in the long term. And as a holistic system, the nadi technique affects the whole person as opposed to the part, and so there is no need to focus solely on the affected part of the body. The treatments are designed to encourage harmony and balance, thereby helping to normalize the body's energy system.

Holistic Principles of the Nadi Technique

As a holistic process, the nadi technique always works on the premise that before you can heal the part, you must first treat the whole. Once it is accepted that the human organism itself is comprised of individual components that collectively constitute a powerful concentration of energy, then healing it becomes feasible. From a metaphysical perspective, when a particular part of the body becomes infected with disease, it very often means that it has become detached from the other components that make up the whole and is therefore no longer connected to the main energy source. Using simple energizing holistic methods, the individual parts of the body may be infused with vitality, thus encouraging a more consistent movement of energy throughout the various channels. The good thing about the nadi technique is the fact that it is comprised of many different healing treatments, so you do not have to rely solely on one method. If one doesn't work, then another will. You could compare the nadi technique to all known antibiotics; when one fails to cure the infection, then another will most certainly be successful.

Working on the premise that the human organism is permeated by a network of channels that convey energy from one part to another in very much the same way that blood is pumped round the body through the veins and arteries, the nadi technique is an effective way of working with the body's energy system, thereby bringing it under control. To achieve this, strategic points in the body are manipulated with the use of pressure, gentle tapping, or even specific hand positions that can either be used in combinations or individually applied, whichever works best for you. Understanding that the mind is very often the common denominator where the health is concerned, the nadi technique also includes mental exercises to help exert greater control over the body and its energy system, as well as specific meditations to encourage inner peace and harmony.

The term *holistic* is today perhaps greatly misunderstood or even overused; some may even think it has religious connotations with a reference to holiness. In actual fact, when applied to complementary treatments, the term *holistic* is the consideration of the *whole* person, and this is exactly what the nadi technique attempts to achieve: it treats the whole as opposed to the part.

The nadi technique is much more than a series of exercises to affect the process of healing; it also involves a core of teachings that encourage a deeper understanding and awareness of the universe and the law of attraction. An understanding of the way in which energy is processed through the nadis and the subtle anatomy will help you gain greater control of the way your body and mind function, and in the long term will improve the overall quality of your life on all levels of existence.

Meditation

Having worked with the chakra system and subtle energies for a little over thirty years now, I began to realize that much more than psychic and spiritual qualities could be achieved with an understanding of how the whole energy system actually works. I had always known that energy can effectively be controlled by meditation, and so I set about creating my own streamlined meditation program combined with certain breathing techniques that brought the whole program together. It worked for me, so I began teaching it to others, with some remarkable results.

It was clear to me that meditation combined with controlled rhythmic breathing is an incredibly powerful healing tool, and although meditation does not suit everybody, the system I had integrated into the nadi technique was easily mastered by everyone who used it. In fact, the nadi technique of meditation was not simply a means of quieting the mind, as it affected the practitioner physically as well as psychologically, and results were also achieved in a very short space of time.

Chakras

Where the chakra system and energy are concerned, I have always advocated experimentation as opposed to what others say is correct. Only then will you have a much clearer understanding of what chakras really are and what energy feels like streaming through the nadis. Although at times my approach to the subject of chakras, the aura, and energy does not comply with the traditional view, as a healing practitioner I realized that it helped quite a lot of people both spiritually and psychologically. Once one has become accustomed to actually feeling the movement of energy in one's own body, it becomes quite easy to control and manipulate the in-pouring energy force and even to direct it to an external location for the purpose of either healing or influencing someone else at a great distance.

Prana

Prana is the term used in Eastern esoteric parlance to describe all energy in the universe. It is an incredibly potent force that is responsible for the maintenance of the body's health and equilibrium, as well as, of course, for the maintenance of balance and harmony in the whole of creation.

When the inflowing prana is restricted in the body, providing there is no serious underlying disease, several visits to an acupuncture practitioner usually remedy the problem. By inserting fine needles or applying electrical impulses to strategic points across the surface of the skin, energy congestion is easily broken down. With the belief that energy crystallizes at strategic points in the feet, reflexology works on a similar premise, and with gentle manipulation at the appropriate points on the soles of the feet, the crystallized energy is broken down and encouraged to flow freely. Apart from this, prana can be controlled with the use of a system of breathing techniques called pranayama, which we shall discuss at some length in chapter 5, but as it is an extremely important part of the nadi technique, I shall be touching on it at various times throughout the book.

A map of the human body is seen by such practitioners as consisting of an intricate network of channels (meridians) along which energy flows from strategic sites to the major organs of the body. As previously stated, any restriction in these meridians produces an adverse effect on the corresponding part of the physical body.

The nadi technique encourages the transportation of energy and much more, and it will enable you to see your body as a map through which to navigate to a healthier, more dynamic life. I have used it with a great deal of success on thousands of people who have been suffering from the simplest ailments to the most life-threatening conditions.

Although I describe the nadi technique as a system of self-healing techniques, it is just as effective when used to heal psychological and physical maladies in other people, as well as to encourage them in the process of spiritual understanding and awareness. At best its treatments will effect a complete cure; at worst they will bring about welcome and much-needed relief.

In my seminars and courses, I have taught the nadi technique to hundreds of other practitioners, many of whom have modified it to suit their own style and technique of healing. Regardless of how it is used, the results are always the same.

Food and Nutrition

The nadi technique consists of new healing methods based on ancient ideas, which I have formulated primarily for the healing of the body, mind, and spirit. What you eat is also considered in the nadi technique, and later in the book, working on the premise "you are what you eat," my wife Dolly has given various examples of power food, with some ideas of food preparation to help with the assimilation of energy nutrients and health-giving properties.

I first met Dolly at one of my seminars in 1998, and she struck me as someone with an incredible spark of originality and enthusiasm regarding the way she perceived food and its nutritional value. She first became interested in the nutritional value of food and its healing properties from a very early age and studied Domestic Science in school. Although at that point she was a meat eater, she knew only too well how important a balanced diet actually was for the maintenance of health. While at college, Dolly secured a job in the catering industry. Her mother's failing health caused Dolly to take an even more avid interest in the nutritional value of food, and as a result she made a concerted effort to transform her mother's diet by encouraging her to eat healthier food. Her mother reluctantly agreed, and a vast improvement in her health was apparent in a very short time.

Dolly began working with me at my center some ten years ago now and has made a significant contribution to the diet aspect of the nadi technique.

Although consisting of a fairly eclectic collection of treatments, the nadi technique also includes the fundamental principles of universal laws and spiritual development that culminate into what the ancient yogic masters referred to as the Path of Attainment. A rudimentary understanding of the spiritual laws that govern our lives will help us to see that we are, in fact, controlled by the same forces that operate within the confines of the universe; and when we begin to change our attitude toward the universe, the universe and all its power will change toward us. In fact, nature never betrays us; we are betrayed by our own blindness: our ignorance.

We cannot ignore the law of cause and effect, which is in constant operation all through our lives. Our thoughts not only produce a corresponding effect upon the way in which our bodies function, but the way we think also has a resonance on the life that we live and everything and everyone around us. The nadi technique lets us see that within us there is an internal universe, and just like the movement of the planets in the heavens and the revolutions of Earth around the sun, the components of which our bodies are constructed are subject to that same universal rhythm. Disharmony with the universe eventually impacts upon our lives and produces disharmony within, causing sickness and disease of varying degrees. The only way to conquer the laws of the universe is by obedience. When we obey the universe, we can then choose from her boundless store the forces that serve our purpose. The nadi technique encourages a much deeper understanding of the numerous spiritual laws that govern our life, and it also considers the planet in relation to the whole system of energy conveyance through its own subtle channels.

Planetary Consciousness and Earth Energies

In 1921, amateur archaeologist Alfred Watkins suggested that ley lines geographically aligned places of historical significance such as ancient monuments, megaliths, natural ridge-tops, and water fords. Watkins further suggested that ley lines had been created in Neolithic times for navigational purposes and ease of traveling, when much of the landscape was then covered with forests. I have no doubt that the theory posed by Watkins is quite feasible, but it does not account for the mystical occurrences that have been attributed to these sacred channels for thousands of years. Today followers of the New Age tradition accept ley lines as being responsible for spiritual and mystical phenomena, with a belief that they are associated with mystical land forms and even feng shui.

In the same way that the body is mapped out with a network of nadis, so too is the planet a matrix of channels relentlessly conveying energy throughout Earth's core, maintaining its health and equilibrium. Unlike ley lines, these subtle Earth channels have a resonance with the nadis permeating our subtle anatomy, a phenomenon that in some way maintains our connection to Earth's more subtle energies. You might say that we are in some way manipulated like marionettes, as our connection to Earth's energies via this intricate network of subtle channels in many ways restricts what we do as well as frequently forces us into situations that are very often out of our control. The planet upon which we live is at all times in control of what we do, and our lives only begin to go wrong when we ignore the subliminal messages passed on to us via these extremely powerful umbilical connections with Earth itself. To all intents and purposes, we are an integral part of an immense planetary consciousness, and the parts we play in the great scheme of things depend entirely on how sensitively receptive we have allowed ourselves to become.

Although today there is still a minority of the human race who have very little regard for the planet, let alone for their fellow man, the collective consciousness of humankind continues to expand, like the swelling waters of a dammed river during a storm.

Just like the human organism, the planet possesses a subtle anatomy too, and although its vibratory tones most certainly equate to the human chakra system, its unique organization creates a different resonance at strategic locations across the uneven terrain of the planet. It may well be that our prehistoric forebears possessed some knowledge of this when they erected their Neolithic and Bronze Age monuments and megaliths at strategic places of burial and worship, and the very reason why temples and monasteries were later erected at specific locations, perhaps where the earth energies were more prevalently powerful. Today little or no consideration is given to where exactly important structures are erected and how the overall ambiance of a location can affect an individual psychologically and spiritually. Would that we could know exactly what our prehistoric forebears knew about the effects of earth energies upon the human consciousness; then the world in which we presently live would no doubt be a much happier and more harmonious place.

The complex network of nadis in our subtle anatomy equates in more ways than we realize to the subtle channels that permeate the planet upon which we live and breathe. It is also via these channels that a rudimentary form of communication occurs between us and the consciousness of the planet. With the passage of time, those with a sufficient understanding of earth energies and how we are subliminally influenced by the planet and the vastness of the universe will be able to access the great reservoir of spiritual knowledge known to the ancients as akasha. The nadi technique is a unique and very easy to follow system that I created primarily to encourage an expansion of awareness to the realization that the planet, the universe, and human consciousness are, in fact, one, and that the external world as we perceive it is transitory and just a great illusion.

The majority of health problems manifest in the body as a direct consequence of the way we have become accustomed to thinking. Our worries, fears, and other negative emotions such as jealousy and envy create poisonous chemicals in our bodies that slowly eat away at the cells from which our whole biology is composed. So, too, in the long term is the planet upon which we live affected, and our attitudes toward other people greatly contribute to both the creation and destruction of the world around us. We must never be too complacent nor underestimate the great law of karma, the law of consequence, or the law of cause and effect, for this law is divine justice and the mighty sword that is forever wielded by the hand of God, the lawgiver. Theology teaches that we are always punished for our sins, but the higher teachings inform us that we are, in fact, punished by our own ignorance and by our own mistakes. Whichever way you choose to perceive it, you are responsible for your own actions, and you are the guardian of your own life.

Overview

The nadi technique has come a long way since I first began developing it into a holistic healing system. Over the years, I have treated thousands of people and taught the nadi technique to other practitioners who use it today, albeit with some modifications. The one essential thing about the nadi technique is that it works on all levels, from the physical to the spiritual points of view, and it also changes the way people think, which is an integral part of the system.

Because in some cases I have modified some of the more widely known pressure points and complementary treatments to fit the nadi technique, it is important not to draw comparisons between them, as the nadi technique is a streamlined system designed to treat specific conditions as well as to encourage holistic balance. Although, as I have previously explained, it consists of an eclectic collection of treatments, they are only similar to other complementary treatments inasmuch as they work with subtle energies and use some pressure points similar to those in other, more traditional treatments. This is where any similarity ends. Much of what is comprised in the nadi technique is the culmination of many years of experimentation.

If you already work as a complementary practitioner, try to be impartial and not look at the treatments too closely. Even the way in which the network of nadis permeates the subtle anatomy may very well not coincide with the view you have of the map of the body. When selecting what treatment to use from the nadi technique, try not to be too analytical or pedantic; the nadi technique requires you to use a great deal of intuition and inner guidance. When treating yourself, it is important to be objective about your body, illnesses, and health conditions. It is also of paramount importance to be experimental and adventurous when selecting a treatment.

With a deeper understanding of the aura and bioluminescence, we will see in chapter 1 exactly how to have a deeper insight into our lives and take greater control of our health. We will explore the historical facts of the aura and look at how the pioneering research conducted by Dr. Kilner and Semyon and Valentina Kirlian was an inspiration to others working in the field of diagnostic medicine.

We will also look at the chakra system and rotational balancing to stimulate the activity of the individual chakras. By infusing the chakras with prana, it is possible to enhance the quality of our health and encourage equilibrium. Here we look at simple but effective procedures to stimulate the subtle energy system, an integral part of the nadi technique. Once this process has been carried out, with the use of a simple arm-pressure testing process, the level of activity in the individual chakras can be tested. After the nadis have been cleared, polarizing the chakras then becomes a straightforward procedure.

In chapter 2 we consider the process of positive thinking, attitude, and calling upon the universe for the things we want to attract into our lives. We will look at how overall health can be effectively maintained by exerting control over the energy flowing through the nadis. This holistic process becomes even more powerful when music is integrated into the treatment, with a look at how the melodic tones of music can sometimes evoke memories of past-life experiences. Here we also make a detailed analysis of how the cells of which the body is composed can be effectively influenced by thought.

In chapter 3 we see how the health of the body can be restored effectively by affecting the movement of prana through the nadis, as well as releasing blockages by mentally distributing prana from one organ to another. When we feel under the weather or even depressed, the simple process of infusing the nervous system will encourage the restoration of vitality and promote calmness and well-being. Here I also explain the nature of the endocrine system and how it can be maintained through mental persuasion, as well as how color can be used to heal the body's ailments and restore equilibrium.

Just as an automobile develops faults in its engine resulting in an overhaul, so too do the body's components eventually break down, necessitating some fine-tuning. In chapter 4 I look at energetic frequency and self-healing by infusing prana with different colored rays. I also explain how the chakra system has a resonance to musical notes, and—just like a musical instrument—will occasionally require some tuning. I also make a detailed analysis of healing and restoring the body's energies with the use of magnets, which also realign the chakra system.

In chapter 5 I look at specific treatments and explain how certain pressure points alleviate common ailments such as anxiety, migraines, and sinus pain. Panic attacks can be instantly stopped with the use of specific power points that can be applied with great ease. By ascertaining the amount of discomfort when tapping the nadis, you can tell how congested they are and, with a specific treatment, alleviate the problem. For anyone suffering from lung congestion or any other discomfort of the chest, specific breathing techniques may be used to improve breathing and release congestion.

Finally, together with my wife, Dolly, we finish the book with a look at the importance of a healthy nutritional diet and how this helps transform our life on all levels of consciousness. Here we also consider the spiritual transformation that is occurring across the face of the planet today.

Because each treatment is complete in itself, there is absolutely no need to use it from beginning to end. Read through the whole book and then select the treatments you think would help you. You may even feel a need to modify or even combine some of the treatments; experimentation is the key word—find what works for you, then use it!

The nadi technique is an extremely effective holistic system that may be used for a broad spectrum of self-development and healing. The only thing that is new in the nadi technique is the way I have formulated it. Its underlying fundamental principles have formed the basis of self-development methods used by ancient masters for thousands of years and were techniques that were regarded almost as sacred. Some of the methods I have integrated into the system are quite straightforward and easy to follow, while others require a little more discipline and practice on the part of the practitioner.

We both wish you a healthier, peaceful, and more spiritual life.

Billy & Dolly Roberts

Medical Note

Please note that the information in this book is not meant to diagnose, treat, prescribe, or substitute consultation with a licensed healthcare professional. Both the author and the publisher recommend that you consult your medical practitioner before attempting the techniques outlined in this book.

I

The Subtle Anatomy
The Chakras and the Aura

In his book *Fourteen Lessons in Yogi Philosophy and Oriental Occultism*, Yogi Ramacharaka suggests that apart from the physical body we also possess other, more refined bodies, each interpenetrating the physical body. They are sustained via an intricate network of channels along which energy constantly flows in the relentless process of maintaining balance and equilibrium. In fact, Ramacharaka refers to our energy bodies as the seven principles of man and says that each one is subdivided into seven, and so on in infinite succession. Man is a multidimensional cosmic being whose subtle bodies extend far beyond the parameters of the visible spectrum. Theosophist Annie Besant also covers the subject at some length in her book *Man and His Bodies* and explains how they are constantly energized by a universal fluid that courses through fine channels (nadis) like blood through the veins.

Apart from these two notable writers, this concept is widely known in yogic circles, and the subject of man's energy bodies is one of the fundamental principles underlying yogic philosophy.

Following this, we understand that the human organism is far more than it appears at a physical level and is, to all intents and purposes, an electromagnetic unit of incredible power, assimilating, modifying, and discharging energy. It is also contained within its own spectrum of light and color. And so the human organism consists of several bodies of varying tones and degrees, each rising in a gradually ascending vibratory scale and each more refined than the one below it. At this present moment in our spiritual evolution, the physical body is the most apparent of our several bodies and is therefore the only vehicle of conveyance available to us while we live on a dense three-dimensional planet.

Just as the physical body consists of innumerable cells, tissues, nerves, muscles, and fibers that collectively constitute the whole, so too is the subtle anatomy composed of energy components of a considerably higher frequency. Although the subtle anatomy is invisible to the naked eye, it is still able to exert powerful control over its physical counterparts. And while the majority of people cannot see the subtle anatomy, those who possess a rudimentary form of clairvoyant vision may be able to see an integral part of it as a colorful haze surrounding the body—in fact, the aura.

Many people wrongly assume that the aura itself is a subtle or energy body, when in actual fact it is a combination of subtle energies that interpenetrate the physical body as well as radiating outward from it into the surrounding space. Each of man's subtle bodies radiates energy, and it is the energy radiating from all the bodies combined that constitutes the aura, a vaporous mass of electromagnetic particles that surrounds every living thing to a greater or lesser degree.

Bioluminescence and the Aura

Bioluminescence is the production and emission of light by a living organism, and it is thought to be the result of a chemical reaction during which chemical energy is converted into light energy. This phenomenon is seen in some deep sea aquatic creatures, and in the human organism it is an external indication as to the degree of internal balance or imbalance, whichever the case may be. In his book *Magic of the Aura*, Bruce Copen explains that in the early 1950s, scientists at Moscow University conducted extensive research into human bioluminescence that led them to postulate there is also a bioplasma body interpenetrating the physical body. They further concluded that this bioplasma body was a sort of "etheric framework" or matrix on which the physical body is constructed, rather like the wire framework on which a sculptor molds his clay. It appeared to the researchers that when the bioplasma body sustained damage as a consequence of inconsistent energy flow, a corresponding effect was produced in the overall condition of the physical body, manifesting as disease. The research was groundbreaking and led to even further investigations into the metaphysical side of the human organism.

The aura is best described as a vaporous mass of electromagnetic particles surrounding both animate and inanimate matter, although the aura surrounding the human form is quite different in appearance. In fact, the human aura exhibits quite an amazing display of color and changes with every thought, feeling, and emotion. Our diet also has an effect upon the color arrangement of the aura, although this effect is transitory and may be equated to throwing a drop of colored paint into a fast-running stream of clear water.

The majority of people have some idea what the aura is, even though they refer to it as simply a haze or glow or even energy around the body. Occasionally we might say that someone has an aura of peace about them or that the house has an aura of peace and calm. But the aura is far more than a descriptive term; as previously stated, it is now a scientific as well as a metaphysical fact. Although it's now fairly common knowledge, in her book *The Piatkus Dictionary of Mind, Body and Spirit*, Paula Byerly Croxon states that the first to actually photograph the aura was husband and wife team Semyon and Valentina Kirlian from Krasnodar, near the Black Sea, who accidentally discovered the technique. The monochrome image produced by the Kirlians' crude apparatus allowed them to make a fairly detailed study of the energy radiating from the fingers and hands. In fact, the Kirlians were the first to conclude that the way in which energy radiated from the body was an indication of internal balance or imbalance, whatever the case may be, and as a result they were able to use their camera as a diagnostic tool. The Kirlians were an inspiration to others working in the same field, and although their camera was quite primitive by today's standards, it was an innovation at the time. Today more sophisticated cameras are used to photograph the whole aura in color, complete with a digital analysis.

In his book *Magic of the Aura*, researcher Bruce Copen explains that in 1911 Dr. Walter John Kilner, a medical electrician who was also in charge of electrotherapy at St. Thomas's Hospital in London from 1879 to 1893, was so fascinated with human energy that he devised a method to make the human energy field visible to the naked eye. This involved a coal-tar dye (dicyanin) injected between two glass plates. When the patient stood behind the Kilner Screen, as it became known, the aura became visible. Kilner's research in the field of human energy led him to write a best-selling book on the subject, titled *The Human Atmosphere* (later retitled *The Human Aura*). Kilner believed that disease could be seen in the aura a considerable time before it became apparent in the body, and he saw his screen as an innovation in the field of diagnostic medicine. In fact, in 1883, twenty-eight years before he developed the Kilner Screen, Dr. Kilner became a member of the Royal College of Physicians and was highly respected by his peers for his pioneering work.

Working on the premise posed by Dr. Kilner and the Kirlians—that disease is seen in the aura a considerable time before it becomes apparent in the physical body—an aura camera would be invaluable in the early diagnosis of disease. However, there is still a lot of skepticism about whether or not what is photographed by an aura camera is actually the aura or nothing more than some form of heat radiation. Nonetheless, if we are to assume that the aura does most certainly exist and can be accurately photographed by a special camera, then it would open up a whole new field in the world of diagnostic medicine.

In fact, the phenomenon of the aura has caused a great deal of controversy over the years and has also been the topic for many debates amongst scientists and pseudo-scientists such as parapsychologists and paranormal researchers. Nonetheless, it still continues to fascinate and intrigue both skeptics and those with an interest in esoteric and metaphysical sciences.

However, what the aura is *exactly* still remains a mystery, even though many theories have been given as to its true nature. It is spoken of by psychics and mediums with some authority, even though what the majority actually see is only a minute part of what there is to be seen. I have made a detailed study of this over the last thirty years and have even tested hundreds of mediums who claimed to be able to see the aura in its entirety. On my television series *Secrets of the Paranormal*, mediums were asked to write down the colors they claimed to see around a selected member of the audience, none of which corresponded. Extensive studies of the human aura have found that it constantly changes and that as well as being affected by diet, it is also greatly affected by circumstances and environment, which also can affect health.

Following extensive studies in the early fifties into the bioluminescence of the body, Russian scientists at Moscow University were convinced that they had discovered the key to making an accurate diagnosis of disease and concluded that all diseases could be detected in the human aura long before they became apparent in the body. More recently, Japanese scientists studying the human energy field developed a device to monitor cryogenic measurements emitted from the body, and after extensive research they concluded that these measurements of varying degrees of heat produced a fairly accurate analysis of the person's health condition at the time.

An Analysis of the Aura

Some observations of the aura show that it is more extensive at the back than it is at the front, and yet the aura of a visually handicapped person tends to be the same all round, looking to all intents and purposes like an egg. This would suggest that it is a sort of radar device and would account for the fact that the hairs on the back of our necks stand up when we feel as though we are being observed from behind. The aura of a visually handicapped person is far more extensive for more or less the same reason—to enable them to safely negotiate their way around obstacles. In other words, the aura also appears to serve as a sort of sensing device and is a metaphysical extension of the senses.

We have all experienced sitting alone in a theater or standing in line when something makes us look round to see someone staring intently at us. You may have even been alone in the house, perhaps preparing the evening meal or tidying the living room, when suddenly you feel uncomfortable, almost as though someone is behind you, watching you. Of course, there is nobody in the house except you; even so, for your own peace of mind, you still feel compelled to check every room, just make quite certain nobody has climbed in through an open window upstairs. As a sensing device, the aura is also capable of monitoring invisible sources, as in the case of a disembodied presence. The aura is multidimensional and, in some cases, can extend several feet into the surrounding space. When you find yourself amongst people whom you don't know or simply feel uncomfortable with, your aura tends to contract somewhat until you become more acquainted with them, at which point it expands to blend with its surroundings.

Although the aura tends to change very quickly with every passing thought and feeling, there is also an aspect of it that is predominant over the rest of it, and this represents the person's true character and nature and therefore never really changes unless some sort of character or spiritual development occurs. The aura is infused with the vital force, prana, and it is this that maintains the health of the body. However, before we take a look at the chakra system, we must first have an understanding of prana.

Prana: The Vital Force

Prana is the subtle agent through which the life of the body is sustained; the more prana that enters and remains in the body, the higher the quality of life. A reduction in prana results in the lowering of your vitality and ultimately a deterioration in the quality of your life. Understandably, where there is no prana, there is no life. According to theosophist C. W. Leadbeater in his book *The*

Etheric Body, prana is believed to be the principle responsible for the integration of the cells into a whole—a sort of binding universal force. As we age, prana has more and more difficulty circulating the subtle anatomy, and so the movement of our limbs is greatly impaired. Eventually prana withdraws completely, and we die. At this point the body slowly disintegrates, and the atoms of which it is composed run amok, taking with them sufficient prana to enable them to retain their vitality and form new combinations. Even with the death of the physical body, there is still life, albeit at a lower level.

Consistently high levels of prana in the body are imperative for the maintenance of health. And through a system of breathing called pranayama, combined with a frugal diet, yogi masters are able to enjoy a long and healthy life. Pranayama is a respiratory process of controlling the inflowing prana and mentally distributing it evenly throughout the body. While prana is in the air that we breathe, it is not the air itself. While it is not matter, it is found in all forms of matter. The animal and the plant kingdoms take it in with the air, and if this energy was not present with each breath, death would occur. And so we can see that prana has its own particular part to play in the manifestation of life, apart from the obvious physiological functions. The powerful streams of inflowing prana need to be controlled, modified, and evenly distributed throughout the body. This process is controlled by the chakra system, to which we will now turn our consideration.

Chakras

The important part that chakras play in the process of modifying and transporting energy in our bodies is very often overlooked. The word *chakra* translated from Sanskrit into English literally means "wheel" or "circle." The majority of New Age devotees have at least a rudimentary understanding of the chakra system and know more or less where they are located on a chart of the body. But as well as the seven major chakras that are considered primary, there are also hundreds of minor chakras strategically located all over the subtle anatomy, supporting the process of controlling the inflowing energy at an even more subtle level.

The seven major chakras with which we are mostly familiar lie across the surface of the etheric body (a more subtle energy body) on the spinal column and are connected to the endocrine glands and nerve plexuses through an extensive system of channels called nadis, mentioned earlier. Chakras are, in fact, sometimes equated with electrical transformers, modifying and controlling the inflowing energy in the same way that electrical transformers help to modify an electrical current, thus lowering its voltage output. Once the inflowing energy has been modified, it is then distributed by the chakras to the major organs of the body, thus helping in the ongoing maintenance of balance, harmony, and the overall health of the body. When viewed from the side, chakras appear like television satellite dishes receiving impulses from the supersensual universe; once their development takes place, they are forced outward so they are able to transmit as well as receive.

Diagnostic Analysis of the Chakras

As with most things in life, each chakra possesses negative and positive qualities, and the dominant qualities are often encouraged by circumstances, environment, opportunity, and upbringing.

When the performance of the base chakra is inferior in any way whatsoever, it is apparent in the person's gait. As an example, when this chakra is exerting a negative influence over the person, they nearly always walk without moving their arms. The positive qualities nearly always make the person hardworking,

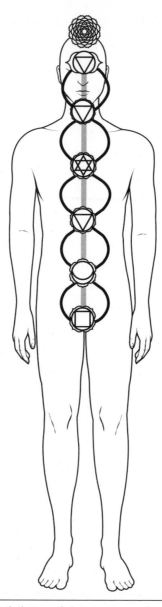

FIGURE 2: *The chakras and their corresponding colors—base (red), sacral (orange), solar plexus (yellow), heart (green), throat (blue), brow (indigo), and crown (violet).*

determined, imaginative, passionate, and loyal. Mediumistic and healing abilities potentially may also show.

When the sacral chakra is exerting a negative control over the person, they tend to walk with comparatively small strides and with little movement in their thighs, regardless of their stature. The positive qualities of this chakra are nearly always mediumistic skills and artistic abilities, with a particular skill for color and design.

When the solar plexus chakra is producing a negative effect, the person looks clumsy and appears not to know exactly what to do with their hands. In fact, the solar plexus chakra makes a person appear nervous and fidgety. The positive qualities of this chakra make the person take control in stressful situations and give them the ability to see things nobody else can see, with a particular skill for resolving difficult problems. The person nearly always shows mediumistic or psychic tendencies.

When the negative energies of the heart chakra are the problem, the person rarely makes eye contact when engaged in conversation and nearly always walks with their eyes to the ground. They nearly always appear shy and insecure, with an obvious lack of confidence. The positive qualities of this chakra are compassion, healing, and counseling, with an overwhelming need to care for anyone who is unwell. This person is a natural healer.

Of all the seven major chakras, the throat center exerts the greatest control over the person. Because this chakra is directly associated with the thyroid gland, it tends to influence the person psychologically and emotionally. Any imbalance in the throat chakra makes a person appear hyperactive and nervous, yet extremely observant and also prone to depression. The positive energies produced by the throat chakra are creative qualities, astuteness, inspiration, clairaudience (the ability to hear super-sensual sounds), and leadership qualities.

When the brow chakra is either sluggish or overactive, this can cause the person to become depressed, lethargic, and lacking in motivation. It may also produce feelings of inferiority, a suspicious mind, and acute anxiety. The positive qualities of the brow chakra are sharpness, intuition, spontaneous inspiration, and the ability to resolve complicated problems. Other inherent properties of the brow center are creative tendencies and a propensity toward the arts.

As I have previously explained, although the crown chakra is mostly dormant at this stage of human evolution, it does show signs of a rudimentary awakening in individuals of a certain degree of spiritual development. Flashes of inspiration and all-knowingness are briefly experienced when the crown chakra is spontaneously activated, albeit very briefly.

Familiarizing yourself with the negative and positive aspects of each chakra so that you can identify chakra and energy problems at a glance will also enable you to make an immediate detailed analysis, a prerequisite when endeavoring to realign energy flow in the subtle anatomy. However, unless you are medically qualified, any diagnostic thoughts should be kept to yourself and used only as guidance when you are administering the nadi technique for the purpose of healing.

Parental, Societal, and Past-Life Programming in the Chakras

There is no doubt that if a child's subtle anatomy could remain untainted all through their life, the world would be a much better place. Unfortunately, from a very early age, a child's mind is programmed by parents who chastise and impose upon the child all the things their parents imposed upon them when they were children. This parental programming eventually causes the electromagnetic polarity of the child's chakra system to change completely, and in so doing it closes down, with all memory of its previous existence lost.

However, in his book *Super Consciousness Through Meditation*, Douglas Baker suggests that chakras are, in fact, cosmic banks containing a record of all pre-life experience. As one develops and the individual chakras begin to evolve, so the experiences from all incarnations are gradually returned to the individual as well. Whether or not this hypothesis is true, one cannot dispute the important part chakras play in our personal spiritual evolution and ultimate manifestation of consciousness. Whatever you believe, you are always in control.

To understand this process more fully, one has to have some understanding of the way in which the individual chakras control our full psychic, spiritual, and creative potential.

In his book *The First Principles of Theosophy*, Jinarajadasa suggests that although the seven major chakras are potentially present at birth, only the one at the base of the spine is fully active. This is responsible for the instincts of the newborn. The baby cries when it is hungry and instinctively moves its mouth toward its mother's breast in search of sustenance. This hypothesis is also posed by Hiroshi Motoyama in his book *Theories of the Chakras*, where he suggests that it takes seven years for the chakra system to fully develop.

First Chakra

This is the first chakra to become active at birth and is responsible for the production of instinct and desire. In adult life, although it controls the lower passions, it is also responsible for hidden strengths and aspirations toward material success. The consciousness of those who live out their lives with little or no thought for their fellow man, possessing no belief in a god or anything beyond the physical world, functions primarily in the root chakra, Muladhara.

Second Chakra

The sacral center, Svadisthana, is the sexual chakra and the "fire" in the human organism. This spleen chakra is full of surprises from which the hero is occasionally seen to rise. The sacral center also contains leadership qualities seen in a president or military person at the battlefront.

When a child reaches their second year on this planet, the next chakra gradually becomes active. By now the child is slowly becoming aware of their surroundings and begins to develop their character as their consciousness functions at this level of awareness.

Third Chakra

The solar plexus center, Manipura, is where it all happens, from a psychic point of view. I consider this chakra to be the motivator or driving force of the individual. This is known as the "sun center" for obvious reasons and is the human epicenter of aspirations, goals, and endeavors. Some refer to this chakra as the "magic" chakra because it is from this center that greatness sometimes emerges.

By the age of three, the influencing energies of the third chakra cause the child to be assertive with determination. Rudimentary creative skills also become apparent at this early stage—more evidence of the energies produced by the third chakra. The child's sensitivity also becomes apparent with this chakra's development. Any imbalance in this center may produce nervousness and mistrust.

Fourth Chakra

A well-balanced heart chakra, Anahata, produces a loving peacemaker and someone with a propensity toward healing. Doctors and nurses who are extremely devoted to their jobs very often possess extremely active heart centers. On the downside, a sluggish heart center means that the person is an emotional wreck, insecure, and very vulnerable.

As the fourth chakra, located in the heart area, begins to unfold, the child's sensitivity (or lack of it) becomes apparent. Now the child is greatly affected by any environmental disharmony and will forever be influenced by memories of this time.

Fifth Chakra

The throat chakra, Vishudda, is connected to the auditory response mechanism. As well as being responsible for the psychic skill clairaudience—the ability to hear disembodied voices—it also controls levels of prana in the thyroid gland, promoting harmony and balance. People with extremely active throat chakras tend to be able to concentrate for long periods of time and are also observant and good listeners.

With high levels of activity, the brow and throat chakras combined bring balance to an individual's life, and once they are perfectly synchronized, they encourage intelligence and success.

Associated with the auditory faculties and the thyroid gland, once the fifth chakra begins to unfold, the child begins to listen and really learn. It's at this time that the child becomes a little person in their own right, and a fairly accurate assessment can now easily be made of their level of intelligence according to the degree of development in this center. The level of development in this chakra may also show a propensity toward the mediumistic skill of clairaudience. Imbalances in this center are sometimes an indication of thyroid problems and minor nasal and throat conditions.

Sixth Chakra

The brow chakra is regarded as the seat of what is traditionally the third eye and is responsible for clairvoyance and other intuitive skills. More than this, though, the brow center, Ajna, is also responsible for inspiration and focus, and those with a well-developed brow chakra are often able to assess and calculate complicated formulas. They are able to think outside of the box, so to speak, and are extremely intuitive.

Apart from being responsible for the powers of concentration and inspiration, the sixth chakra is also responsible for the psychic gifts of clairvoyance and intuition. Imbalances at this center may also cause depression, migraines, and other minor neurological conditions.

Seventh Chakra

The chakra at the crown of the head, Sahasrara, is associated with God consciousness. Although this chakra is dormant in the majority of the human race, it shows a rudimentary form of activity in those who devote their lives to prayer and meditation, such as some monastic orders, mystics of the highest kind, and Tibetan masters. Occasionally we have glimpses of this chakra when we feel as though we have been touched by some divine force and helped from a critical situation. Sahasrara is also believed to be the boundless reservoir of all knowledge from which scientific researchers, doctors, writers, and artists receive their inspiration, albeit briefly.

In his book *The Advanced Course in Yogi Philosophy*, Yogi Ramacharaka suggests that the seventh chakra is dormant in the majority at this stage of evolution and only shows signs of development in those who devote their lives to prayer and meditation. However, the seventh chakra is our direct connection to universal consciousness, which is the primary reason why in monastic communities the tonsure was a prerequisite for godliness.

And so the chakra system evolves at a rate of one a year, appearing to all intents and purposes like minute flowers, the petals of which increase as they ascend the spine. And so when the child reaches seven years old, their chakra system is fully formed and the aura untainted. In fact, according to C. W. Leadbeater in his book *The Chakras*, he described the development of the seven major chakras as appearing "vivified like coruscating whirlpools of color and vitality."

If you feel that you are creative but find yourself somehow prevented from expressing your full potential, the chakras should be checked to ascertain whether or not any of them are sluggish or even inactive. Sluggishness in the chakra system can occur for many different reasons and may be caused by anything from poor diet to stress and even wrong thinking.

Instead of focusing your attention on the offending chakra, the whole chakra system should be treated. If this doesn't resolve the problem, then you need to focus your attention on the chakra responsible for preventing you from achieving your aims. One would assume that an individual whose life is influenced solely by the root chakra would have no interest whatsoever in raising their consciousness to other chakras. However, regardless of which chakra one's consciousness is influenced by, all the chakras can be collectively or individually developed, thereby releasing the inherent potential of the aspirant.

There are innumerable misconceptions about chakras and the way they can be treated. One common misconception is that they can be opened and closed, rather like the shutters on a portal of some sort. We have already established that they are spiraling vortices of microscopic energy. Just like our complexion, the color of some chakras can become anemic and drained of its vitality. This usually comes about as a consequence of the body being abused with alcohol, nicotine, or a poor diet. As well as maintaining harmony and balance in the aura, the chakras also help with the distribution of pranic energy throughout the subtle and the physical bodies. From a metaphysical perspective, chakras connect one subtle body to another, and it is at each of these points that pranic energy passes through the various nadis in the never-ending maintenance of life.

Now we can begin to fully understand the complex nature of the subtle anatomy and see the chakra system as an immense system for the modulation of energy. As I have said elsewhere, the human organism is an electromagnetic unit of immense power and is contained within its own spectrum of color and light. Even a rudimentary comprehension of all this will give you some idea in which direction we are heading where the nadi technique is concerned, and once you have experienced the concept of energy, you should then be able to formulate your own method of manipulating energy for any purpose whatsoever.

Although we are now exploring the chakra system as an integral part of the subtle anatomy, it is important to understand the concept of energy and how the chakra system controls that. So, before we move any further, to give you an idea of what prana looks like when it is seen in the aura, you may like to try a little experiment. For this you will need two apples and a piece of white paper.

NADI TECHNIQUE I: *Seeing Prana*

First, remove some of the pips (seeds) from an apple. Place the pips on the piece of paper and simply gaze at them.

Once your eyes have become accustomed to staring at the pips, you should see a pale blue or even white haze around them, most probably moving around the brown pips with a clockwise motion. The haze should appear to stream from the pips quite evenly.

Remove the pips and place them in an envelope for a few hours. After this time, return them to the white paper and gaze at them again. You should now see that the haze around the pips has changed somewhat and appears depleted and not as vibrantly bright.

Now remove some fresh pips from another apple, and then place three or four of these around the old pips on the piece of paper. You should then gaze at all of them to witness an incredible phenomenon. It will appear as though the energy from the new pips is reaching out to the old pips, seemingly in an asserted effort to revitalize them. You may even see the energy from the old pips attempting to reach out to the vibrant energy of the fresh pips.

The old pips represent a sick person depleted of energy, and the fresh pips are like a healthy person full of vitality.

This little experiment allows you to see what the aura looks like at a lower level. The energy that you see around the pips equates to what is generally thought of as the "health" aura and is that aspect of the human energy field that shows the level of vitality present. Although usually much more vibrant when seen in the human aura, this is an extremely effective way of knowing exactly what prana looks like when it is emitted from a living organism.

Pressure Points and Visualization

Well-balanced chakras encourage a consistent and even flow of prana along the nadis. In the same way that the arteries can fur up and clog, causing problems with the heart, so too can the nadis become congested if the health of the subtle anatomy is not maintained. By exerting mental control over the nadis and visualizing the energy moving through them as one continuously free-flowing pool of water, the levels of prana may be maintained and encouraged to flow freely. This may be easily achieved with some simple exercises combined with applying a little pressure to specific points on the body. These will be covered later.

NADI TECHNIQUE 2: *Charging Water with Prana*

Although water is a conduit for prana, the amount of prana in it can be increased or infused with specific colors for the purpose of treating a particular health condition.

First of all, to increase the levels of prana in a glass of water, simply pour it from one tumbler to another, backwards and forwards, over and over again for at least one minute or until the water sparkles and appears to be alive. To enjoy the full benefits of the energized water, it must then be consumed immediately.

Water may also be infused with specific color rays to increase its vibratory tones. For this you will need seven drinking glasses, each one in a color of the spectrum or, alternatively, seven sheets of thin, transparent plastic (to allow the light to pass through it), each in a color of the spectrum. These can easily be made into tubes, taped or stapled, and then placed over the glass of water.

Then it all depends on the nature of the health condition you are going to treat. For example, should you have a high temperature, the water should be poured into a blue glass and then left on the window ledge in the warm sunlight for at least an hour. To prevent anything from falling in the water, you would be advised to cover the top of the glass.

The solar rays charge the water with the vibratory tones of the color, increasing the potency of the pranic content and encouraging its natural healing force. The glass of water may then be kept in the fridge and consumed when required. However, if the water is kept in the fridge, to ensure the potency of the prana is maintained, subject it to the pouring process discussed above before drinking it.

Alternatively, when the temperature is low, a red glass may be used to infuse the water. A full list of colors and their tonal values can be found in chapter 3.

Water charged with prana should be consumed after every exercise. This encourages the precipitation of prana through the nadis.

NADI TECHNIQUE 3: *Rotational Balancing*

Occasionally we all feel out of sorts or under the weather, whatever you choose to call it. Feeling out of balance is more often than not a simple lowering of the body's vitality, and usually a good night's sleep puts things right. However, when the stresses of life overwhelm us, we need far more than a good night's sleep, particularly when the stress is caused by an unavoidable situation. It is now common knowledge that stress is one of the biggest killers, and the condition itself contributes to many other life-threatening diseases, from heart attacks to cancer.

Before attempting rotational balancing, you will need to first practice your hand coordination, which may prove challenging for some people. However, once you have mastered the technique, you will find the process extremely invigorating, and you can then use it whenever you feel in need of a pick-me-up. If you find it difficult to master the rotational hand movement on your-self, then engage the help of a partner to apply the treatment.

The procedure moves energy strategically along the nadis pre-cipitating the chakras and produces an invigorating effect upon your whole body. For the most effective results, the treatment ideally should be applied to the points of the body where the chakras are located; in this way, not only will the chakras them-selves become infused and polarized, but the movement of prana around the body will also be encouraged. It is this that causes feelings of invigoration and elation, making the mind sharp and the body feeling as though it has had a powerful tonic.

Although in a healthy person energy is constantly being pro-cessed through the subtle energy system without any restrictions at all, when we are out of sorts or suffering from any type of ill-ness, the transmission of energy through the nadis becomes slug-gish. To encourage the energy processing to be more consistent and restore your vitality, initially the treatment should be admin-istered at least once every day for one or even two weeks. Should you see an improvement in the condition after only one treat-ment, you would be well advised to carry on for the period sug-gested above. You could equate this to the advice given by your physician to complete a full course of antibiotics even if you feel better before you've used the entire prescription.

Whomever is being treated should lie in a horizontal position with their eyes closed and a cushion to support their head. (The same applies even when treating yourself.)

Beginning with the head, hold the left hand (fingers spread wide apart) about 2.5 cm away from the head, making sure not to touch it, and your right hand on top of the left, without touching, also approximately 2.5 cm away from the head.

Slowly rotate your left hand with a clockwise motion, and rotate your right hand with an counterclockwise motion. (You should now see why coordination is important.)

Spend no more than one minute on the forehead before slowly moving your rotating hands down to the throat area, again without actually touching the body. It is imperative that the hand rotation is consistently maintained as you slowly move down to the area of the heart. Rushing the process defeats the whole object of the treatment, which is to evenly distribute prana through the nadis of the individual chakras.

It is more effective to allow yourself to be intuitively guided to the locations of each chakra, as this is often more reliable than following the traditional locations of the chakras (as seen in the chakra chart on page 36).

Apply the rotating hands to all the chakras, from the forehead to the genital area in the base chakra.

Having completed the rotational treatment, apply the process in reverse, from the genital area back to the forehead.

At the conclusion of the treatment, your partner (or yourself, if you were practicing alone) should drink a glass of charged water (in nadi technique 2) to ensure that the body is fully hydrated. This encourages the movement of prana along the nadis, thus promoting harmony and balance in body, mind, and spirit. The psychological benefits of this treatment alone are immense, which is why it is extremely effective where depression and related illnesses are concerned.

You will have noticed that I have not included the crown of the head in the treatment. As previously explained, the crown chakra is considered dormant in the majority of people at this stage of evolution, and therefore it does not require any treatment. However, if you choose to include the crown chakra in the rotational process, it would not do any harm and may even complement the whole treatment.

Although not absolutely necessary, a little visualization of swirling energy while rotating the wrists may help the facilitation of the force in the chakras and through the nadis.

For maximum results to be obtained, the rotational balancing treatment should be sequentially followed at least three or maybe four times in one session, more if you feel a need.

Once you fully understand the concept of energy and the way the body's equilibrium is maintained by it, you should then be able to see with much more clarity how its levels may be increased and then manipulated for reasons ranging from heightening awareness to encouraging the holistic healing process in the treatment of all diseases.

NADI TECHNIQUE 4: *Infusing Exercise*

Here is another extremely effective way of controlling prana in your own body for the sole purposes of easing pain and increasing your vitality. It is perhaps one of the simplest methods I know.

Sit on a straight-backed chair with your eyes closed and your hands resting lightly (palms down) on your lap.

As with other exercises, breathe rhythmically until a rhythm is fully established, making sure that the inhalations and exhalations are evenly spaced.

When you feel quite relaxed, place your left hand on top of your head and your right hand on the base of your spine.

Continue to breathe rhythmically. When you notice a change in the temperature of one or both hands, transfer your left hand to the base of your spine and your right hand to the top of your head. Allow them to remain in that position while you continue to breathe rhythmically.

When you notice a temperature change in one or both hands, repeat the previous process and switch hands. Continue this procedure for approximately ten minutes and then relax with your hands on your lap. Remember to keep your eyes closed all through the exercise, as well as maintain the slow, easy rhythm of your breathing.

This exercise infuses the nadis with prana and encourages the precipitation of vitality in each individual chakra. It is an ideal pick-me-up when you are feeling under the weather. It is also extremely effective for easing many painful or inflammatory conditions such as migraines or arthritic problems.

Although the exercise is extremely effective using just your hands, it can also be done holding clear quartz crystal points in each hand. Because of its geological properties, clear quartz enhances the energy in anything close to it. In this case the crystals encourage the precipitation of prana through the nadis, producing a sort of washing or cleansing effect on body, mind, and spirit.

For an additional option, use different crystals—for example, the milky quartz is the female, and the clear quartz is the male. For the purpose of this exercise, hold the milky quartz in your left hand and the clear quartz in your right. This corresponds with the major male and female nadis, ida and pingala. However, using male and female quartz is not absolutely essential, and two clear quartz points will still produce positive results.

NADI TECHNIQUE 5: *Testing the Chakras' Vitality*

Muscle-pressure testing is something that anyone who knows about kinesiology will be familiar with. This is a simple yet extremely reliable method that can be used to assess the performance levels of the individual chakras, which will then give you a fairly good idea of where treatment is needed on the body. For obvious reasons, this test requires two people.

If you are the person being tested, stand up straight with one arm horizontally extended in front, the hand closed into a fist, and your other arm by your side. Although not absolutely essential, ideally your writing arm should be extended.

Resist the pressure as your extended arm is sufficiently pushed down by the second person to ascertain the strength in it. This will help to accurately compare strength when testing the chakras.

Take a moment to rest the arm before continuing to the next part of the experiment.

The exercise should now begin with your arm again extended in front of you. This time you should place the other hand on the forehead, between your brows, while resisting the pressure as your extended arm is pushed down.

Make a note of any apparent changes in the strength of the extended arm. If it shows signs of being weaker, then this is an accurate indication that the brow chakra is sluggish and requires treatment.

Repeat the exercise with your hand placed on the throat. Once again, make a note of any changes in the strength of the extended arm. This will help you to ascertain the level of activity in the throat chakra.

Repeat the process with your hand placed on the area of the heart, then on the chakra just below the left side of the ribcage, then in the area of the naval, and finally at the lowest part of the trunk, in the genital area, noting any changes in the strength of the extended arm.

You may notice that sometimes your extended arm becomes even stronger. This is also an extremely accurate indication of the level of activity in that particular chakra and would suggest that the corresponding skills of that chakra, either psychic or creative, are quite strong. It should also be borne in mind that the chakra system can be greatly affected by your overall health, and any inactivity may not necessarily be permanent.

NADI TECHNIQUE 6: *Polarizing the Chakras*

Even from a scientific point of view, you can see that the human organism is an electromagnetic unit of incredible power and is contained within its own color source, a spectrum of varying degrees of color energy. The human body is an amazing piece of machinery that is hard-wearing and designed to withstand all the traumas that life throws at it. As I have explained elsewhere, chakras are also small, transformerlike units controlling, modifying, and distributing the constant streams of inflowing prana in much the same way that electrical transformers modify and control currents of electricity in the maintenance of electrical circuitry.

The individual chakras either can be treated with the rotating hand method or with a treatment such as stimulating the nadis with the use of clear quartz crystal points accompanied by some gentle manipulation. While moving the crystal points along the body with one hand, without actually touching the body, make a massaging motion with the other hand, following the crystal point along the same route. The use of clear quartz as an energy enhancer was an integral part of many ancient therapies, particularly those practiced in Egypt and India. Clear quartz is a powerful and much-underestimated substance that is used in industry for all manner of different things, particularly for maintaining the intricate precision of watches. It is thought that the advanced race of the legendary city of Atlantis powered their homes with crystals and that it was crystal power that eventually brought about Atlantis's ultimate destruction.

Let us first of all take a look at the use of clear quartz as a means of treating the chakras and the nadis. Working on the holistic premise that we are treating the whole as opposed to the part, the treatment should be applied to all the chakras in sequential order, beginning with the root, or base, chakra. For the treatment you will need two clear quartz points, one male and one female. As explained previously, the female quartz is cloudy and the male absolutely clear. Alternatively, if you have difficulty obtaining quartz points, any two pieces of quartz will suffice.

As with previous procedures, the treatment is most effectively applied with the person in a horizontal position, face down. This makes for easier, unrestricted access to the individual chakras.

The person doing the healing should hold the female (cloudy) quartz in the left hand and the male (clear) quartz in the right hand. Hold the point of the female quartz over the top of the male quartz, with the point of the male quartz directed at the base chakra. Without touching the person, slowly rotate the clear quartz in a clockwise motion and the female quartz in an counterclockwise motion. Make certain that the female quartz is held over the male quartz at all times. In fact, spend a few minutes on this point, increasing the time by one minute on each chakra. (It may be a good idea to practice your coordination a little before beginning the treatment.)

Treat all the chakras with the male quartz rotating in a clockwise motion and the female (cloudy) quartz rotating in a counterclockwise motion, taking care to rotate the crystals slowly and increase the time spent on each chakra by approximately one minute as you ascend the person's spine. I have already explained that chakras look, to all intents and purposes, like small flowers, with the petals on each increasing as they ascend the spine. This treatment will increase the intensity of the chakras, and for a time feelings of disorientation may be experienced.

Once you have applied the treatment to the throat chakra, the same should be applied to the brow center through the back of the skull, concluding the treatment at the crown of the head. Once the crown of the head has been treated, the whole process should be reversed, from the crown back down the spine to the base chakra. Although I have not included the crown chakra in previous treatments, involving it in this treatment encourages polarization of the whole system and promotes balance and inner harmony.

Although positive results are usually obtained on the first treatment, to maintain balance the whole treatment should be repeated at least once a week for a month.

This is one of those treatments that must be tried to be believed. It is an extremely effective way of clearing and cleansing the nadis and is a tonic or pick-me-up when recovering from surgery or illness.

Remember, the word *chakra* means "wheel" or "circle" in Sanskrit, and so it is unnecessary to open and close them, as many people believe. It is enough to activate each individual center, thus causing them to collectively become infused with vitality.

See figure 1 on page 10, showing the position of major nadis. Although the subtle anatomy is permeated with an intricate network of nadis, the three major nadis that are considered primary—ida, pingala, and sushumna—play an extremely important part in maintaining the equilibrium and overall balance. The ida and pingala nadis regulate the male and female (or the yin and yang principles), making you who and what you are. Too much yin or yang causes imbalance and lack of focus, as well as an inability to achieve and take control of one's life. Regularly treating the chakras and the nadis in the above way encourages overall balance and helps in the maintenance of all the subtle parts that culminate into the sentient, self-aware being that you are, as well as the spiritual and cosmic person that you will one day become. Treating the chakra system and the subtle anatomy in this way encourages balance in the male and female energies and helps to control negative energies such as aggression, anger, impatience, hate, and anxiety.

NADI TECHNIQUE 7: *Clearing the Primary Nadis*

Although I have given various methods of cleansing and clearing the channels here, this technique encourages balance in the three primary channels, ida, pingala, and the central spinal channel, sushumna.

These three nadis play an extremely important part in the manifestation of male and female consciousness. The central channel, sushumna, is responsible for the assimilation and transportation of prana from the base of the spine to the brow.

The pingala nadi is the male energy and is symbolized by the sun; it is referred to as "ha" in esoteric parlance. Although this nadi is located in the right nostril, it controls the left side of the brain. The ida nadi is the female aspect and is symbolized by the moon. This is referred to as "tha" in esoteric parlance. This nadi is located in the left nostril and controls the right side of the brain. Both of these nadis cross the central spinal channel, sushumna, in a serpentine manner, constantly transporting pranic energy from the chakras to the organs of the physical body. You may have already noticed that the words *ha* and *tha* are a direct reference to hatha, those physical disciplines of that particular branch of yoga. *Hatha,* roughly translated, means sun and moon, male and female, and *yoga* means union—unification, or bringing together the male and female or opposites, encouraging harmony and balance on all levels of consciousness.

Although the method given here to clear the three primary nadis is extremely simple, it is a most effective one and should not be dismissed purely on its simplicity. It requires no visualization and virtually no effort at all for it to produce positive, immediate results. This nadi technique produces an invigorating effect upon the mind—ideal for when you are exhausted or simply not feeling the best.

Sit on a straight-backed chair and follow the same procedure given in previous exercises, ensuring that the chest, neck, and head are in as straight a line as possible, with the shoulders thrown slightly back and the hands resting lightly on the lap.

Follow the previous routine of breathing rhythmically until a rhythm is fully established, thus encouraging the mind to be quiet.

To infuse pingala, the male nadi, simply place the two middle fingers of your right hand against your left nostril, closing this with a little pressure, and place the palm of your left hand on the right side of your abdomen.

Having completed this, with your eyes closed, breathe in through your right nostril, holding your breath for the count of six, then exhale, again holding your breath for the count of six. Repeat this four times and then relax, with your hands resting lightly on your lap.

To infuse ida, the female nadi, place the two middle fingers of your left hand against your right nostril, closing this with a little pressure, and place the palm of your right hand against the left side of your abdomen.

Having completed this, breathe in through your left nostril, holding your breath for the count of six, and then breathe out, again holding your breath for the count of six. Repeat this four times before relaxing with your eyes closed and your hands resting lightly on your lap.

As you become more proficient, you can increase the retentions to slightly longer periods.

Another effective way to do this nadi cleansing technique is to inhale for the count of six, retain the breath for the count of three, and then to exhale for the count of six, count three between breaths, and so on.

Whichever way you carry out the exercise, the palm on the side of the abdomen is an essential part of the procedure, as it encourages the precipitation of pranic energy through the chosen nadi.

Remember, it is not necessary to use every single method in the nadi technique, as each procedure performs its own particular holistic healing function. It is advisable to try every method at some time or another, though, so you will have a pretty good idea of which methods work best for you.

As always, drink a glass of water after pouring it backward and forward from one glass to another, over and over again, until it seems to come alive.

One of the fundamental principles of the nadi technique is the cultivation of positive thinking. Even though the power of the mind should never be underestimated, we are only as strong as our weakest thought. The mind is very often the common denominator where the health of the body is concerned, and a positive attitude should always be adopted when treating illness of any kind.

2

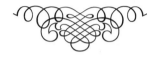

Dynamic Thinking

You may be wondering what the nadi technique has to do with dynamic thinking and how your subtle energies can possibly have an effect upon the way you think. We have already established that thoughts are, in fact, living energies, and these energies originate somewhere deep within the consciousness. The intricate network of nadis that permeates the subtle anatomy is responsible for the control and ultimate transportation of prana, and in order for balance to be maintained in the subtle anatomy, it is of paramount importance that this process continues unrestricted. Both the health and vitality of the physical body, as well as the strong thoughts we release, are maintained by the constant, vital flow of prana through the nadis.

The millions upon millions of thought waves produced by each individual attract and are thus attracted by thoughts of a similar nature. They form "thought strata" in psychic space in pretty much the same way that clouds fall into groups in the atmosphere. Each stratum of thought is of different degrees of vibrations, and so the same space may be filled with thought matter of a thousand kinds, passing freely and interpenetrating each other without interference. In other words, each individual draws to himself thoughts corresponding with those produced by his own mind, and he is, of course, in turn influenced by those thoughts. For example, should you dwell upon something for any length of time, be it good or bad, it will seem as though all nature has conspired to lead you into a position whereby your thoughts can be gratified. These are the fundamental principles of the great law of attraction, a law which is both right and just.

Thought Power

You are the architect of your own destiny simply by the way you think, and the way you have become accustomed to thinking is more than likely the way you are. Buddha once said, "You don't get what you want, you get who you are!" To understand this aphorism more fully, you must first of all have an understanding of the fundamental principles underlying the laws of thought.

Without a doubt, thoughts are living things; the stronger the thoughts, the more energy with which you charge those thoughts. The more energy present with each thought, the longer it will persist in the psychic space. This being so, you are continually populating your own private portion of space by the way you think. As we have seen in previous chapters, the mind exerts an incredibly powerful control over your body, and your thoughts send electrical impulses to the innumerable groups of cells of which your body is composed.

In more ways than we realize, the way we think is responsible for our health and equilibrium; negative thinking ultimately produces poor health, and a positive attitude creates a healthy body. Today the majority of people know this but are usually not in a position to actually do anything about it. Worry is something we all experience at some time in our lives, but according to the fundamental principles of thought, the more we dwell upon something we fear, the more we attract it into our lives. If this is the case, then under that same law we can call toward us all the things we desire. The universe is never wrong and all things are possible when we bring about radical changes to the way we think. This is far easier said than done, yet by applying yourself each day to some carefully constructed mental exercises, you will be amazed at how such a transformation can be brought about quickly.

Biology of Meditation

As a means of enhancing the quality of their lives, many people dismiss meditation on the grounds that it is either too complicated or it is for certain kinds of people. In all actuality, anyone can meditate, and it is far from complicated, requiring as little as ten minutes of your time each day, longer if the mood takes you. Apart from the obvious health advantages of meditation, there is also the incredible effect it has on the subtle anatomy and the nadis.

It is now the general consensus of opinion amongst medical practitioners that meditation in any form is good for the health. Although the value of meditation has been known through antiquity, the theory really only became fashionable in the 1960s when it was presented to the world by the Maharishi Mahesh Yogi, an Indian physicist who developed a meditation technique he called Transcendental Meditation, or TM as it is now known. This method of meditation involved the chanting of a mantra, or a special word that was personal to the meditator. When chanted for even a short length of time, the meditator would experience a state of euphoria, calm, and serenity. However, even then meditation was regarded as being for certain kinds of people, most probably because it became extremely fashionable amongst the followers of the so-called "flower power" cult of the 1960s. The Maharishi's popularity grew, and TM clinics were opened worldwide. Little wonder, then, that the Beatles became devotees of the Maharishi, attracting even more followers of Transcendental Meditation.

For thousands of years, meditation has been an integral part of most religions and esoteric traditions and was favored by Hindu and Buddhist priests as the only way of achieving spiritual enlightenment and attaining nirvana, the highest state of meditative bliss. With the belief that meditation encourages concentration and promotes calmness and a more even temperament, today meditation is integrated into the educational curriculum of many schools in India. Scientific research has shown that Transcendental Meditation can reduce stress, lower blood pressure, and, in many cases, also anesthetize the body to pain.

In the early 1970s, Dr. Herbert Benson, a cardiologist at Harvard Medical School, made a detailed study of the effects of Transcendental Meditation on its practitioners (Benson 2000). He was impressed by the way heart and respiratory rates became slower and how relaxed the practitioners were, even though they were fully awake. His research led him to develop his own form of meditation, which he prescribed for his patients.

Apart from the medical value of meditation, what else can be achieved with its use? Meditation is the tool of all great minds and the only effective way of reaching higher states of awareness. Meditation encourages the release of certain chemicals in the brain, particularly endorphins, the body's natural pain-relieving hormones that also encourage feelings of euphoria. Meditation is known to have a powerful effect upon the endocrine system, particularly affecting the pituitary and pineal glands. It also encourages the precipitation of prana along the nadis and thus helps to break down any blockages in the major channels, the meridians. Certain forms of chanting can produce similar states to those experienced with some hallucinogenic substances, which is most probably why many ancient and obscure cultures used hallucinogens to hasten this transcendental experience. In fact, hallucinogens were believed to open the major channels in the subtle anatomy, thus causing the seven primary chakras to be vivified. Needless to say, there are safer methods, and the use of hallucinogenic compounds to achieve this state is most certainly not recommended.

More recent reports suggest that building bigger and more efficient brains lies in the practice of meditation. These conclusions were reached by a group of researchers from the University of California—Los Angeles, who used magnetic resonance imaging (MRI) to scan the brains of people who regularly meditate. In a study published in the journal *Neuroimage*, the researchers claimed that certain regions in the brains of long-term meditators were actually larger than those of a similar group. Specifically, meditators showed significant enlargement in all regions of the brain responsible for regulating emotions. "We know that people who consistently meditate have a singular ability to cultivate positive emotions, retain emotional stability, and engage in mindful behavior," said Eileen Luders, a postdoctoral researcher at the UCLA Laboratory of Neuro Imaging. "The observed differences in brain anatomy might give us a clue why meditators have these exceptional abilities" (*Neuroimage* 2009). In addition to having better focus and control over their emotions, many people who meditate regularly have reduced levels of stress and increased immune systems. Less is known about the link between meditation and brain structure.

In the study, Luders and her colleagues examined 44 people: 22 control subjects and 22 who had practiced various forms of meditation. The length of time they had been meditating ranged from 5 to 46 years, with an average time period of 24 years. More than half of all meditators said that deep concentration was an essential part of their practice, and most of them meditated for between 10 and 90 minutes each day. The researchers used a high-resolution three-dimensional form of magnetic resonance imaging by which they could not only divide the brain into several regions in order to study size but also compare the amount of gray matter within specific regions. They found significantly larger cerebral measurements in meditators as well as increased gray matter. There were no regions where the control group had significantly larger volumes of gray matter than the meditators.

In the same article, Dr. Luders is quoted as saying, "There might be underpinnings that give meditators the outstanding ability to regulate their emotions and allow for well-adjusted responses to whatever life throws their way." She also suggested that a further study would be required on a microscopic level to discover why meditators' brains develop in a way that other peoples' do not. She also noted that numerous previous studies have pointed to the brain's remarkable plasticity and how environmental enrichment has been shown to change the neurological activity.

These remarkable studies are just a few of the many that prove that meditation is most certainly good for health.

Hallucinogenic Compounds and the Mind

The ancient Aztecs and other cultures used peyote, a globe-shaped spineless cactus from which was extracted the extremely hallucinogenic compound mescaline, which they imbibed to encourage higher states of consciousness. The so-called Mushroom People built their entire religious tradition around *Amanita muscaria*, which they referred to as the sacred mushroom. From it they extracted the hallucinogenic compound psilocybin, also used by shamanic priests in their magical rituals.

The pineal gland, one of the endocrine glands, is greatly affected by hallucinogens. These encourage activation of a minute part of the brain that is normally dormant, thus precipitating higher states of awareness. Shamanic priests and other ancient cultures no doubt understood this and had to undergo the vitally important process of spiritual development before they would even consider imbibing the powerful hallucinogens. These sacred substances were imbibed only by those who were spiritually qualified and able to mentally access other dimensions where they could receive direct communication with their dead ancestors.

In time, meditation produces the exact same results as hallucinogenic substances, and it is the only means by which one can safely reach higher states of consciousness. Meditation also encourages the release of melatonin from the pineal gland, which thus precipitates the electromagnetic waves from the crystalline deposits surrounding it, encouraging the pine cone–shaped gland to act as a sort of neurological radar system and allowing it to receive data from the supersensual side of the universe. This data may either include flashes of inspiration or the ability to receive communication from a disembodied source, as in the case of a medium. There is very little doubt that, practiced over a long period, meditation heightens awareness by increasing the sensitivity of the faculties.

On a more practical level, meditation is an ideal tool with which to overcome stress and alleviate the symptoms of acute anxiety. However, the meditation technique that suits one person may not in any way suit another. Some individuals have little or no problem focusing the attention for any length of time, while others have minds like butterflies and find it completely impossible to focus the attention for more than a couple of seconds.

Therefore, a meditation program needs to be created for the individual, with consideration given to their overall personality and general temperament. A hyperactive individual who suffers regular anxiety attacks will most probably find it difficult to sit quietly for long periods and so will need to be introduced to a series of relaxation exercises before meditation is integrated into their training program.

As someone who used to suffer with an anxiety neurosis and was programmed to have a panic attack every single day, I know only too well how important it is to learn the art of relaxation, particularly when the body has grown accustomed to being tense and has learned to panic at certain times and in specific situations on a regular basis. A relaxed body and a quiet mind are prerequisites before meditation even can be considered. Trying to meditate when the mind is anxious merely defeats the whole object of the exercise. Although I have been teaching various meditation techniques for thirty years, I have integrated it into my daily program for a little over forty years. In fact, at one point in my life meditation really helped me, and although the technique of meditation I use today is not the one I used all those years ago, it is still an integral part of my daily training regime.

As explained above, for thousands of years artificial means have been used to induce altered states of consciousness, when the safest and most effective way is meditation, the tool of all great minds. In fact, for many monastic bodies, meditation is the highest form of prayer and an extremely powerful way of elevating the mind to that transcendental place of God consciousness.

Apart from mistakenly believing that meditation is for certain kinds of people, more individuals than you might imagine abandon their interest in meditation because they believe it is far too complex a system to master. In its defense, therefore, I must say that meditation is only as complex as you yourself make it. It can be as simple as sitting in the armchair and staring into the flames of a roaring fire. If the technique of meditation you have employed works for you, then that is the one that you should use. If your needs change, your meditation practice can too.

Although in the 1960s the use of meditation was almost a fashion accessory and a prerequisite for many "flower power" followers, it has since been realized that meditation has a holistic effect upon the health and even encourages longevity. It is for this reason that I decided to explore meditation and help you find the correct method for you. In the following pages we will take a look at several methods of meditation, with an accompanying guide to relaxation and techniques for improving concentration.

The process of meditation has been integrated into many ancient religious and philosophical traditions, and it has always been regarded as an extremely safe and very effective way of raising the consciousness into transcendental states of awareness. There is nothing strange or weird about meditation, but its effectiveness is dependent upon dedication, patience, and a disciplined nature.

Living Life in the Fast Lane

Living as we do in this so-called fast and modern age of science and technology, there is little wonder that stress has become the number one cause of most diseases. These range from heart disease to migraines, anxiety neurosis to cancer. Few people really know how to relax and have wired their bodies always to be in a prepared state of mind, ready for action. Relaxation is alien to a lot of people whose adrenaline levels are frequently so high that they live perpetually in a psychological fast lane. Of course, it goes without saying that living life in this way is like walking through a biological minefield, and it is just a matter of time before the health explosion occurs. I am speaking from pure experience, and I learned very early on the importance of getting into the habit of "turning off" on a regular basis, particularly at night, when my batteries need to be recharged.

The nadis are biologically programmed to follow your orders and may be greatly influenced by integrating some visualization into your meditation program. In fact, when the image-making faculty of the brain is involved in meditation, even in a rudimentary way, the body's reservoirs of prana may be precipitated to such an extent as to encourage the self-healing process holistically. Even the simplest of mental imagery can exert a strong influence over the cells of the body, causing their rearrangement when there is an abnormality of any kind. In fact, visualization techniques are used in many cancer clinics to complement the traditional treatment of the disease; meditation and visualization should never be underestimated.

NADI TECHNIQUE 8: *The Process of Focus*

The mistake the majority of people make when attempting to use the power of thought is to make too many demands at once. It is just like a child asking Santa Claus for lots of different presents, when in reality it is far better if they ask for just one thing they desperately want. This may sound ridiculous, but sending too many demands at once to the universe merely defeats the whole object of the exercise and causes a short circuit to occur. We are not talking about praying to God here, although one could say that using the power of thought to obtain the things or the help you need could be considered as being the highest form of prayer.

Learning to relax should be an important part of the process, as this encourages the mind to be more focused. For this part of the process, it is not absolutely necessary to sit in a disciplined position, although it is important that you are not so comfortable that you are in danger of falling asleep. Once you have mastered this technique, you should find that your consciousness has been taken to another place—a zone where all sense of time is lost.

Sit comfortably on a chair of your choice. You may even prefer to lie on the bed. Whatever position you choose, make every effort to maintain your focus on the exercise.

Relax as much as you can and, with your eyes closed, commence breathing rhythmically, making sure that the inhalations and exhalations are evenly spaced.

Once you are fully relaxed, allow your mind to drift from your breathing until you become completely unconscious of it.

Although it is virtually impossible to empty your mind completely, make every effort not to focus on any particular thought that passes through your consciousness. In fact, focus your attention on the point between your eyes.

Look upon this part of the exercise as being like a child daydreaming, fixed on one point but at the same time not thinking of anything in particular.

Maintain this for at least ten minutes, although if you have fully mastered the technique you should have lost all sense of time. Continue this focusing process until you become aware of your surroundings once again. At this point you will know that the exercise is to be concluded. In other words, do not force it or make it a labor as this too defeats the whole object of the exercise.

Create the feeling that you know it will work, and be consistent all through the exercise with a sense of achievement driving you forward. Some people find it difficult trying to focus their attention on a point of nonthinking, so if you are one of those people, music may be integrated into the program primarily to prepare you for the next step.

The Effects of Music

In 1966, Professor Hans Luftermier conducted scientific research on the effects of music on the human psyche. He concluded that music is most certainly integrated into our biological makeup and that our genetic components are actually encoded with music, making us who and what we are. In fact, even though we humans have taken millions of years to evolve into the sentient, self-aware beings we are today, music has always been there in some form, tightly woven into virtually every culture across the planet.

Not only does music have a profound effect on the brain, but it also has a significant washing or cleansing effect on the bioluminescence of the aura, thus making it more stabilized and together. Music produces theta brainwaves—similar to those in deep relaxation and stage one of sleep—and encourages the process of calmness and serenity.

For many people, music can be just as effective and more therapeutic than the process of meditation. Music has an extremely calming effect on the brain and central nervous system; it absorbs our attention, distracting our thoughts from worries and anxieties. Music consistently inputs the brain with mental stimuli, encouraging the sensory receptors to close down for a while, thus allowing our body to relax and the mind to be quiet.

Music also encourages pleasurable memories to surface and, although there is no definite scientific evidence for it, it may even evoke memories of past-life experiences within the DNA. You may have experienced this without actually realizing what it was. Perhaps you were relaxing, listening to a beautiful piece of music, when suddenly abstract images flashed through your mind, or perhaps mental impressions of picturesque scenes or even faces completely unknown to you spontaneously appeared in your consciousness. These are nearly always dismissed without thought and attributed to the stimulation of the imagination brought on by deep relaxation—but are they?

Of course all music is different, and some we may even find irritating. Some music stimulates the brain and stirs the body into activity, while other more serenely composed music has the effect of calming and quieting the mind and encouraging sleep. Therefore, the correct music has to be chosen in order to affect the mind and make it more quiescent. In fact, music produces long-term effects on the bioluminescence of the body's subtle energy system, and studies at Moscow University in the 1960s have shown that music can heal a broken or fragmented energy system and even encourage a more consistent flow of vitality and color to the overall look of the aura.

Modern research into human psychology has proved beyond doubt that stress and wrong thinking can impair the quality of the health as much as a poor diet. Not only does meditation encourage positive biological changes, but it is also known to improve the way the mind processes thoughts and feelings, thus improving the health. For these and many other reasons, integrate music into your self-healing program. You may like to use it in the following way.

NADI TECHNIQUE 9: *Music as a Meditative Tool*

Play the music of your choice and relax in a comfortable chair.

For the first part of the relaxation session, focus your attention on your breathing. Breathe in and out from your diaphragm, ensuring that the inhalations and exhalations are evenly spaced and that the tummy rises as you breathe in and then falls as you breathe out. This is the correct way to breathe and ensures that maximum benefits from the process of respiration are achieved. The expansion of the chest, as the majority of us were taught at school, is most certainly the wrong way to breathe, as it restricts our intake of oxygen and inhibits the circulation of prana through the nadis.

Spend at least ten minutes (longer if comfortable) on the process of rhythmic breathing, and then relax, with your eyes closed. Sit quietly and allow the music to create images in your mind, perhaps even transporting you to far-off places. Allow the music to totally absorb your attention. Feel it filtering all the stress from your subconscious mind and overwhelming you with that much-needed sense of peace.

Listen to the music for as long as it takes to encourage your body to be relaxed and your mind to be quiet. If you don't feel up to meditating after your period of listening to music has finished, then leave it. Do not under any circumstances force yourself to meditate, as this would only defeat the object of the whole process. Use music to "turn off" from the stresses and strains of the day and to encourage relaxation and quietude. In fact, once you have successfully practiced the entire nadi technique and applied it effectively to your life, you may then feel like formulating your own program using music as a sort of bridge from one aspect of it to another.

The actual psychological process of listening to music is an ideal way of eliminating mental chatter and in itself is a recreational procedure that may be considered meditation. In fact, anything that absorbs the attention and transports the consciousness into other places can be defined as "meditation." Besides all these benefits of music, it also produces an incredible holistic effect on body, mind, and spirit.

Now that the mind is more or less prepared, let us explore the art of delivering your request to the universe by using an extremely simple yet precise and effective method of what I call universal streaming.

NADI TECHNIQUE 10: *Universal Streaming*

Those who make every effort to use the power of thought to obtain the things they want usually abandon it because it does not work fast enough for them. This attitude defeats the whole object of the exercise. When focusing, there is a technique that requires consistency and the belief that it will work. In fact, results may be produced in a fairly short time, and if it takes a little longer—so what! As long as it works, what does it matter? The length of time is not important as long as you achieve your goal.

Universal streaming is a way of ordering your desires, dreams, and wishes before sending them forth into the cosmos. Sufficiently powerful, they will—in accordance with the great law of attraction—create an immense magnetic vortex to pull into your life the things you have requested. As with anything worthwhile, practice most certainly makes perfect. However, apart from your patience and determination, very little effort is required to achieve successful results. There is nothing new in speaking to the universe. As well as being a process that comes within the parameters of quantum physics, it is also a psychological process that Buddhists and ancient adepts have been practicing for thousands of years. Of course, it won't happen immediately and it must be done slowly and in stages.

I have already explained that music may be used to prepare the mind and evoke emotions to rise from the subconscious regions of the mind. This process is not only invaluable to the mechanics of universal streaming, but it is also extremely effective in the practice of self-healing.

Try to see your external life as simply being the result of the way you think, or the culmination of all your thoughts. Every thought results in an action, and every action produces an effect. This makes sense! However, many of our thoughts are quite trivial and possess little or no energy whatsoever, and so they simply dissolve into the ether. Thoughts that have been created out of concentration, passion, desire, and need are perpetuated by the pranic energy that enveloped them upon their release. These become living forces of incredible power and are sustained by the energy with which they were created in the first place.

Sit comfortably on your chosen chair, with your chest, neck, and head in as straight a line as possible, shoulders thrown slightly back and your hands resting (palms down) on your lap.

As you have done in previous exercises, breathe rhythmically until the rhythm is fully established, making sure that the inhalations and exhalations are evenly spaced. Continue breathing in this way for at least ten minutes, taking care not to strain it or make it a labor, as this may cause hyperventilation (overbreathing).

Now, allow your mind to drift from your breathing until you become almost unconscious of it. Gradually allow what it is you want from the universe to come into your mind, and try to see it as though it is already in your possession. Feel a sense of joy and achievement. Take care not to add confusion by focusing on more than one thing at a time. If you are focusing on a situation you are endeavoring to bring about, feel it as well as see it as though it is already something you have achieved. Spend as long as is comfortable on it. Do the same if it is an object you desperately want—feel as though it is already in your possession.

The process is very much like what you did as a child when daydreaming about something you desperately wanted. See it clearly in your mind. Avoid using the process selfishly, as this defeats the whole object of calling upon the universe. Remember the precept that curses and blessings come home to roost.

Successful results are not going to be achieved immediately, so you really do need to be patient and persevere. It may even take you a little time to establish the technique of focusing, but once this has been achieved, results will be achieved.

It may be helpful to look upon this method of channeling your thoughts as a form of prayer. However, instead of humbly asking for the thing you want, by focusing your energies in a systematic, consistent way, you are effectively establishing a firm connection with the universe and commanding it to serve your purpose. This is one of the fundamental principles underlying the process of positive thinking. Although, strictly speaking, it is not meditation, it is a creative tool used in meditation and is designed to cultivate a more dynamic mental force.

The following exercise takes things a little further and requires a more involved approach through visualization. In this first exercise you sent out the mental request through the process of what I call universal streaming, and this should be followed by creating a "mental grotto" from which you can actually retrieve the things you are requesting from the universe. This creates a bridge of consciousness and helps to solidify the things you are seeking to attract into your life, making them far more tangible and real in the many dimensions of the mind.

NADI TECHNIQUE II: *Creating and Entering the Grotto*

As already established, visualization is an extremely powerful and effective mental tool. Although some visualization exercises are childishly simple, they are nonetheless effective and can produce remarkable results in a very short time. For this reason, visualization should never be underestimated.

Look upon the image-making faculty of the mind as an incredible tool capable of shaping its way through the swirling mass of the cosmos with the sole intention of creating the things you want to attract into your life. The grotto is a simple visualization exercise that requires ten minutes (longer if you can) of your time each day.

Sitting comfortably with your eyes closed, once again breathe rhythmically, making sure that your inhalations and exhalations are evenly spaced.

When you are ready, see in your mind's eye a magnificent grotto set in the rocks at the foot of a mountain. Although the grotto is completely empty, it is constructed of brightly colored rocks that seem to glitter with a light that breaks up into myriad colors cascading down in a breathtaking display.

Allow your thoughts to drift away from the grotto for a few moments and establish in your mind what it is you want to attract into your life. Obviously, if you are wishing for a situation, a change in circumstances, or simply to be happy, you will not be able to actually *see* these, but you should be able to feel them. Remember to create the feeling that you have already achieved what you want, and for a moment allow yourself to be over-whelmed with the excitement.

Dwell upon whatever it is you want and feel the grotto filled with the thing you desire. Remember not to fill it with more than one thing, whatever it is, as this merely confuses the universe, and later it will seem as though the whole process has been abandoned.

It is paramount that you interact with the exercise. If it is money you are seeking to attract, then see it in the grotto and see yourself actually holding it. If it is something like a change of circumstance, such as a new job or moving to a new house, then feel as well as see yourself in the new environment, overcome with happiness.

It is essential that your mind does not drift from the exercise even for a moment, and that the feeling of happiness and the sheer excitement of already being in possession of what you want is felt. In this way you empower it and give the imagery life.

Remember not to strain or make it a labor, as this will also create negative energies and will only defeat the object of what it is you are endeavoring to achieve. In fact, visualization should be a joy and looked upon as an exciting experience.

Exerting mental control over prana, the universal energy, encourages mental and spiritual development as well as maintains balance and harmony in the body. A healthy, active mind produces a healthy, active body.

Influence of Thought on the Health

There is very little doubt that the way we think ultimately has a profound effect upon our health. If, as the old saying goes, we can think our way into an early grave, then it must be equally true that we can think our way into a long and healthy life. The way we think also affects all those with whom we come into contact; thought precedes action, and every action produces an effect. Although the majority of people are familiar with the law of karma, only a minority fully understand exactly what it is. Although it includes the law of cause and effect, the implications of karma are far more extensive. Whether we realize it or not, it is in constant operation all through our lives, and it transcends every single thing that we do.

The mind is the common denominator, simply because the way we think is the way we are. We are most certainly the architects of our own destinies, and we shape our future circumstances by the way we think as well as with our dreams and aspirations. It is not so easy to think in a positive way when you are being pulled along by one problematic situation after another, but once the realization dawns upon you that you have the power within to radically change your life and thus pull you from the dark mire in which you are living, the transformation immediately begins to occur.

I am talking from pure experience and know firsthand just how such a transformation can be brought about, even with the smallest change in attitude. In fact, when you change your attitude toward things and other people, things and other people will then change toward you. The universe is never wrong, and once you realize this and learn to work with it, nature will then lead you into a position whereby your dreams and aspirations may be gratified. The weak man must become strong himself and cannot grow from the strength of someone else. Even in his darkest hour he is always the master; even then he possesses the power to direct his mind from the darkest shadows to the brightest landscape. The man who is determined very quickly cultivates the will of a warrior whose sights are set on victory and who does not see defeat as an option.

There is something deep within the minds of us all that possesses the power to attract wealth, good health, and happiness. Those who live in misery and who accept poor health as the way their life has to be have not as yet glimpsed the beautiful light on the horizon of the soul and will forever remain imprisoned by the way they think. Once a man ceases to complain and commences to search diligently for the hidden justice that regulates his life, from that very moment he has set himself free and will have already begun to take control of his own destiny.

You may criticize someone for doing an injustice to you, but the truth is both you and the perpetrator of the injustice are cooperators in ignorance and while seeming to afflict each other are, in reality, afflicting yourselves. The aphorism "as a man thinketh in his heart, so is he" touches every aspect of a person's life. And even though your lips may not have converted your thoughts into words, you are still a slave to all that constantly persists in your mind.

The way you think produces a corresponding effect upon every cell of your body and is also an indication of exactly who you are. A man's features always reflect the way he thinks, and the way in which he has become accustomed to thinking eventually produces a sympathetic resonance with his community as well as with all those with whom he shares his life. A little consideration of the fundamental principles of thought should very quickly allow you to see just how logical all this really is. We all know how we feel after a fit of rage. An outburst of anger affects every nerve, tissue, fiber, and cell of our body and leaves us feeling totally exhausted. In fact, after such outbursts of rage, it really does take some time before our heart rate settles and our skin cools down. Even then, physiologically and psychologically, the effects of the outburst are still felt. Although jealousy leaves us feeling very much the same, this negative emotion produces other feelings, such as sleepless-ness, agitation, and irrational behavior. These negative emotions are all like poison to our bodies and as a consequence produce significant biological changes that ultimately affect our health. It makes a lot of sense that if our emotions really do affect the cells of our body, then with the use of the same mental process the opposite effects can just as easily be achieved.

Let us take a look at how exactly we can influence selected parts of our body with some persuasive mental dialogue. Yes, you've got it: how you can mentally persuade your body to recover from the disease that is causing it so much pain and discomfort. It is possible to exert sufficient control over your body to will it to heal itself.

We have all experienced mental chit-chat from time to time, that silent dialogue that occurs between you and yourself, usu-ally when you are annoyed with someone or even when you are just trying desperately to reach a conclusion about a problem. Of course, such mental dialogue is completely under your control and is a process that we all use from time to time to let off steam, so to speak. But the same process may be applied to heal your body.

The individual components of which the whole of your body is comprised are minute intelligences communicating with each other as they go about their relentless job of maintaining balance, individually and collectively. You are the master of your own body and therefore have the power to make demands and exert control over every minute part of it. You can talk to the individual cells of your body as easily as you can talk to anyone else. Just as your anger, happiness, and joy are apparent to other people, so too are these emotions felt by the individual cells of your body. Little wonder, then, why the cellular structure of the human form frequently runs amok, causing disease and even death. Let's take a look at the simple nadi process of talking to the individual parts that make up your body.

NADI TECHNIQUE 12: *Cellular Persuasion*

It really does help this process to have a background of gentle, soothing music. This encourages the mind to be relaxed and calm.

Close your eyes and mentally scan your body, beginning with your forehead and face, then neck, shoulders, chest, and tummy, all the way down your legs to your toes.

As you mentally go over your body, soothe away all the tension from it and allow yourself to sink completely into the chair or bed, whichever the case may be. In other words, let go and relax every muscle, fiber, nerve, and cell. And as you relax, become aware of your breathing, making certain that it is slow and even. Above all, don't in any way strain your breathing. Relax your body to the extent where you feel warm and tingle all over.

When you are sufficiently relaxed and the mind is quiet and serene, begin sending a mental command to all the cells in your body, particularly in the area of your anatomy that is affected by pain or disease. In fact, begin by addressing the cells of your body collectively, almost as though you are speaking to an audience.

If it helps you, visualize the cells of your body as a sea of faces in front of you.

Be firm and persuasive, but above all be positive. Let the affected part know exactly who the boss is and who is in charge. "I want you to pay attention and listen carefully to me: *I want harmony to be restored.*" Make sure the mental command is forceful and positive.

It doesn't matter what dialogue you use in this part of the process as long as it is positive and forceful. Let the affected cells know you mean business and that you want harmony restored. You may even look upon yourself as a mediator attempting to restore peace to a hostile crowd.

When you feel that you have everything under control and have restored order, to ensure that the affected cells are infused with vitality and that you are fairly certain they have responded to your command, a little visualization should now be applied.

Even though you may or may not be familiar with the anatomical formation of the cells in your body, see them as perhaps minute armies of ants attacking and eating away at your flesh, and then visualize streams of intense white light saturating your body and restoring order once again.

Once you have brought the groups of cells under the control of your will, maintain the visualization of the intense white light for a little longer, then relax.

It is of paramount importance that you do not lose control of the mental imagery and that it is maintained throughout the exercise. If you allow yourself to be distracted for a single moment, the effects of the imagery will be lost. As with many of the other exercises, you should not strain at it or make it a labor, as this only produces unsatisfactory results. After all, it is far better and more productive to spend five effective minutes on the exercise rather than spend a longer half-hearted period that achieves nothing whatsoever. To achieve maximum results, repeat the exercise at the very least twice a day, more if time permits. Also, make certain that there are no distractions during the treatment, as focus and concentration are important.

By exerting control of the movement of prana through the channels, you are able to totally change the polarity of your life, improving your overall health and encouraging a more dynamic approach to everything you do.

3

Affecting Pranic Movement

We have established that the mind is a powerful computerlike unit capable of incredible things. The phrase "mind over matter" is frequently used to encourage us to take our mind away from the discomfort of pain. "Think of something other than the toothache" we are told when that long-overdue visit to the dentist is causing that decaying tooth to cause discomfort. After all, it's the mind that registers pain, not the nerve in the gum, so why can't we use the mind to intervene? That makes sense, don't you think?

Several of the minor nadis pass down each arm and through the fingers of both hands. By gently manipulating the fingers of the right hand, you are able to relieve pain anywhere on the left side of the body, and by applying the same process to the left hand, pain in the right side of the body is then relieved. It is extremely effective and very easy to achieve.

As we now know, the body is a carefully mapped-out chart containing a network of minor and major channels; the major channels are referred to as meridians and the minor channels, nadis. Combined, they help to vitalize the subtle anatomy, maintaining its equilibrium on all levels of existence. If the flow of prana through these channels is in any way restricted, then it will have an effect upon the corresponding parts of the physical body.

Think of the water in a fast-flowing stream en route to the wider expanse of a lake, and the water from the lake thus being pushed to the more extensive river, and so on. Although a simple analogy, it explains perfectly well how energy is conveyed unrestricted from one channel to another. However, if beavers create a dam to prevent the water moving from one of the fast-flowing streams into the wider expanse of the lake, although some water will still manage to filter through into the river, the restriction of the dam will ultimately produce an unexpected effect on the overall flow of the river. The same laws of rhythm apply to the flow of energy in the body as with the flow of water from one source to another. Once you grasp this concept, you begin to have a good understanding of the nature of the ebb and flow of energy throughout the major and minor channels of the subtle anatomy.

NADI TECHNIQUE 13: *Finding Energy Blocks*

Imagine you are holding a soft rubber ball in each hand. Squeeze the imaginary balls as tightly as you can, making a fist with your hand and at the same time making a mental note of any sensation you may feel at another site in the body. For example, the pressure of the right hand may produce some sort of sensation on the left side of the neck. This is nearly always a good indication that there is a slight blockage at that particular point. The same applies with the pressure produced by the left hand. Although you may not have had any particular symptoms of a health problem, in time the blockage will cause something to occur.

When you are squeezing the imaginary balls in your hands, make certain that the ends of all your fingers are digging into the fleshy parts of the palms of both hands, as though you were watching an exciting or frightening movie. This alone stimulates the various nadis in those locations.

NADI TECHNIQUE 14: *Remedy the Blockage*

Regardless of the location of the blockage, to remedy it, simply snap the tips of the fingers quickly into the fleshy parts of both hands, as you would when using a rubber ball to exercise the muscles in your hand. Repeat this as quickly as you can, over and over again and not stopping until you feel either warmth or tingling at the location where you first experienced the sensation. This is an indication that the congested energy has been released.

Remember, the right hand controls the left side of the body and the left hand, the right side of the body.

There are, in fact, numerous ways to encourage the flow of energy in the body; some involve a mental process and others physical manipulation such as the one previously given. The following simple method encourages the flow of prana through the respiratory system, facilitating its distribution. It also helps to ease tension and promote relaxation. You may have to practice this a few times until you fully understand what to do.

NADI TECHNIQUE 15: *Respiratory Distribution of Prana*

Sit comfortably on a straight-backed chair, making sure that your chest, neck, and head are in as straight a line as possible, with your shoulders thrown slightly back and your hands resting lightly on your lap.

As we have done in previous exercises, breathe rhythmically for a few moments, making certain that the inhalations and exhalations are evenly spaced.

When you feel quite relaxed, extend both arms at more or less "twenty past eight" (120 degrees/210 degrees, respectively), with the fingers of both hands spread so that a little tension is felt in each hand and up the arms.

Simultaneously rotate both hands (turning on the wrists) and arms to the right as far as possible, including as much of the upper arm as you can in the rotational process. Take care not to strain them, and then rotate them to the left. Repeat this no more than four times, as any more than this may needlessly dissipate the force. Also make quite certain that the rotational movement is consistent throughout the treatment, and then allow your arms to fall down to your sides and relax.

Breathe rhythmically as before, ensuring that you feel quite relaxed, with the inhalations and exhalations once again evenly spaced. Although this procedure helps the assimilation of prana in the lungs, it encourages a release of tension across the chest and shoulders as well.

NADI TECHNIQUE 16:
Infusing the Nervous System with Prana

Now, folding your fingers firmly into the palms of your hands, making a fist, place the nails of your four folded fingers against your solar plexus. The knuckles of both hands should gently touch each other while the thumbs of both hands point upward to your chest.

Once in position, take a deep breath, hold it while closing the thumbs together, and then exhale. Once all the air has been fully expelled from your lungs, hold the breath while pulling the thumbs apart once again, then breathe in deeply a complete breath, and so on and so forth. Repeat this several times, then relax.

You should notice a calming effect almost immediately. Practiced at least once a day, it will help you to feel more in control and less prone to panic in stressful situations.

Once you have mastered the exercise, you should then introduce some visualization into the process. Repeat the exercise again and visualize streams of intense white light coming into your lungs; on the retention mentally see it circulating through your chest and stomach, and on the exhalation imagine it being discharged as gray fumes. To achieve maximum results, make certain that the imagery is maintained through the exercise.

Exerting control over the nadis in this way also helps to discipline the mind. The mind is really an unknown quantity, and by involving it in the process of visualizing the inpouring energy, you then will be able to direct it to any part of the body where it is required.

In the following exercise, you will be directing the inpouring prana to the head for the sole purpose of easing tension. However, once you are familiar with the process, energy may then be directed to any part of the body where healing is required, or even to another person for the purpose of easing their aches and pains.

NADI TECHNIQUE 17: *Inhaling and Directing Prana*

As with previous exercises, sit on a straight-backed chair, making sure that your chest, neck, and head are in as straight a line as possible, with your eyes closed and shoulders thrown slightly back.

Place the fingertips of both hands on your solar plexus and slowly breathe in for a complete breath, mentally seeing the inflowing breath as streams of intense white light.

When the breath is complete, hold it while transferring your fingertips to your forehead.

Now, slowly breathe out, seeing the intense white light streaming from your fingertips and filling your head completely. When your breath has been fully expelled, hold it while returning your fingertips to your solar plexus.

Repeat the process several times or until you feel a warm or cool tingling feeling either in your hands or your forehead. This is a positive indication that prana is moving rapidly through the nerves, tissues, and cells. Once you have mastered this technique, you can then direct prana to other parts of your body and then into another person for the purpose of healing all kinds of maladies.

The nadi technique transcends the parameters of physical experience and touches upon far more than healing the body. It produces spiritual balancing that helps to polarize your personal energies as well as encourage heightened states of sensory perception. It also helps to precipitate the individual chakras, thus causing their individual colors to be intensified and their vitality to be fully restored.

The Effect of the Endocrine System

You should now have an understanding of the way energy is distributed through the nadis and how it may also be directed to the organs of the body with the sole purpose of revitalizing them. This is the fundamental principle underlying the holistic nadi technique and the whole object of this healing system. We have already discussed how the human organism is an electromagnetic unit of immense power—appropriating, assimilating, and discharging energy—and how it is contained within its own spectrum of light and color. Therefore, the efficiency of the body as a whole is, to all intents and purposes, dependent upon the individual parts of which the whole unit is comprised. Should a single part of the body cease to function effectively, then the efficiency of the rest of it is greatly impaired as a direct consequence. Although we have explored the subtle anatomy—the chakras—and the part they play in the maintenance of bodily health and the evolution of consciousness, we must now turn our consideration once again to the endocrine glands and nerve plexuses, and explore the integral part they play in pranic movement and the general health and well-being of the physical body.

According to *Grey's Anatomy*, the endocrine glands play an extremely important part in the holistic health of the body, and the overall personality of the individual is, to some extent, regulated by one or the other of these glands.

The endocrine glands are sometimes referred to as ductless because they have no ducts and secrete their hormones directly into the bloodstream. These glands, in fact, collectively form the so-called endocrine system, which directly corresponds with the chakra system, and vice versa. As I have already said, the overall health of the body is dependent upon the efficiency of the endocrine glands, and the inefficiency of one of these glands will impact the others.

The endocrine system is comprised of the pineal and the pituitary glands, located in the cavity of the skull; the thyroid and parathyroid, situated near the larynx at the base of the neck; the thymus, situated in the chest above the heart; the pair of adrenals (or suprarenals) topping the kidneys almost like tiny hoods; and the gonads of the male and female reproductive systems. All the endocrine glands are closely related; they supplement and depend upon each other. The healthy functioning of the endocrine glands is of paramount importance to the well-being of the individual, and the minute secretions of hormones from each are responsible for the development of the genius as opposed to the imbecile or the restricted growth of the dwarf as opposed to the giant or even the release of happiness as opposed to sadness. In fact, the endocrine glands exert an incredible influence over the growth of our bodies and the development of the workings of our minds, and in more ways than one they really make us who and what we are. Their pervasive influence affects everything we do, and they not only help to determine the shape of our body but also affect the way we think and behave.

The Pituitary Gland

The pituitary gland is very often perceived as the most important gland, and it has been described as the gland that "gives the tune to all other glands," which appear to be totally dependent on it. In fact, the pituitary gland encourages and controls the inner mobility and efficiency of the whole system; it promotes and controls the growth of the body, glands, and organs, including sexual development. It supervises and maintains the efficient performance of the various structures and helps in the prevention of excessive fat accumulation. A happy, uncomplicated individual without any obvious hangups is nearly always indicative of a healthy, active, and normal working pituitary gland.

The Pineal Gland

The pineal gland is a pine-shaped gland deep within the brain. This is usually larger in a child than it is in an adult and is marginally more developed in the female than it is in the male. The pineal gland appears to harmonize the internal environment. It supervises the development of the other glands, thus maintaining their synchronicity and polarity in relation to each other. The pathological condition of the pineal gland is believed to exert a strong influence over the sex glands and causes the premature development of the system as a whole. In the pineal gland's normal condition, it promotes harmony and efficient functioning of the endocrine system.

The Thyroid Gland

The inner activity in the endocrine system is controlled by the thyroid gland, ensuring that the tissues are fully active, with no water retention, and that there is no densification of bones. The general condition of the thyroid is responsible for whether a person is very active or lethargic, tired or energetic, alert or depressed. The thyroid also controls the development and function of the sex organs.

The Parathyroid Gland

The overall stability of the functioning within our body is, to some extent, influenced by the parathyroid gland, which maintains metabolic equilibrium by supervising the balance, distribution, and activity of calcium and phosphorus in our system. The healthy performance of this gland results in poise and tranquility.

The Thymus Gland

When puberty is reached, the actual size and importance of the thymus gland is reduced, as the part it previously played in supervising natural growth and development should by then have been successfully achieved. The shrinking process of the thymus gland ensures that the natural adjustment of the individual is not impaired.

The Adrenal Glands

The inner vitality and energy is encouraged by the adrenal glands, which drive action, perception, activity, courage, and vigor. The adrenal glands encourage oxygenation of the bloodstream, intensifying this process with revitalized power.

The Gonads

The phenomenon of attraction to the opposite sex is largely the result of healthy gonads of the male and female reproductive systems, whose primary function is to maintain that attraction by encouraging the personality to radiate with confidence and self-assurance. The release of hormones from the gonads encourages inner warmth in the system, ensuring that flexibility is maintained and that the overall health and vitality continues.

To some extent, the overall health and vitality of the endocrine system is maintained by the regular distribution of the life force, or prana, throughout the entire organism. A little understanding of the way in which this life force permeates the subtle channels should enable you to more effectively supervise the healing treatment and thus facilitate the whole process more efficiently.

NADI TECHNIQUE 18:
Mentally Encouraging the Individual Endocrine Organs

Although the very notion of actually communicating with the individual cells and organs of the body does not come within the parameters of conventional medicine, it is perhaps one of the oldest and most effective forms of healing, and one that was favored by yogic mystics of antiquity. As with the nadi technique of speaking to the cells of the body, the process is quite simple and involves dialogue between you and the various parts of your body. The process involves mentally encouraging the distribution of the vital force through the individual endocrine glands, ensuring that each one is revitalized.

Although this nadi technique process involves a little visualization, the primary part of the treatment is the mental dialogue. Simply mentally pass on to the glands the desire for them to be healthy and full of vigor and vitality. You should spend some time mentally scanning your body and willing the individual organs that have been described to integrate harmoniously with the whole.

Once you are satisfied that sufficient time has been spent on the endocrine glands, you can then direct your attention to any affected part of the body, thus applying the same treatment. This treatment should take at least an hour, so it is vitally important that you are reposed in a comfortable, relaxed position. Although this method of healing requires some effort on your part, the benefits are quite remarkable and may be seen almost immediately on conclusion of the treatment.

As always, after the treatment you should ensure that your body is well hydrated by drinking a glass of freshly charged water using the process of pouring from one glass to another as described previously.

Prana and Color Therapy

Although we have spoken at some length about prana, it is nearly always very loosely defined by the majority of people as the vital force. More than this the majority of healing practitioners don't really know. However, we have already established that prana is the subtle agent through which the life of the body is sustained, and the more prana we can retain in our bodies, the better the quality of our health. When recovering from illness, Victorian physicians always prescribed a holiday in a certain seaside resort where there was something in the air that would aid recovery. For thousands of years, it has been known that that certain something in the air is, in fact, prana—an extremely important source of vitality that sustains all life on the planet. It is more prevalent in certain geographical areas, particularly by the wide expanse of the sea.

In fact, water is an extremely effective conduit for pranic energy, and the saline effects of sea water produce incredible streams of prana into the air. Although science has its own theories as to why sea air is good for you, from a metaphysical perspective it is the streams of prana present in the sea air that invigorate the lungs and nervous system. Air and water combined create an extremely powerful healing agent that aids recovery from illness.

Earlier, we learned how to increase the vibratory tones of water with the use of colored drinking glasses. But apart from this process, color may be used in various ways to intensify the inpouring prana from the sun.

NADI TECHNIQUE 19: *Colored Light Therapy*

According to Edwin Babbitt in his book *The Principles of Light and Color*, the ancient Egyptian therapists knew practically everything there was to know about the harmonics of color and how color could be used to cure all forms of disease. According to the ancient practitioners, color produced a resonance in the body and encouraged harmony and balance. They believed that all diseases were the result of depletion in the body's color reserves, and that by systematically infusing the person with the appropriate colors, the condition would be cured.

The ancient Egyptian practitioners of color therapy used different-colored gauze or voile, which they would secure across an opening on the roof to filter the sun's rays and direct them to the affected person. For example, should the patient be lethargic—perhaps as a consequence of depression—a blue filter would be used initially, followed by a green one. Blue is an excellent color for restoring the body's vitality, and green produces a harmonizing effect upon the cells of the body. The treatment would then be concluded with a red filter, thus infusing the patient's body with energy and vitality. Because the vibrations of red can cause anxiety and anger in an individual who is exposed to it for too long, the red filter was only used until the patient's pallor became rosy.

To help you understand the vibratory potency of color, here are some examples to use as a guideline:

Red: The vibrations of red are extremely effective in the treatment of anemia, hyperthermia, and lethargy. Red is also an energizing color that will revitalize the body when you are recovering from illness. Its tonal effects help to increase the levels of prana in a depleted system and will provide instant energy when required. Too much exposure to red vibrations when a person suffers from anxiety can increase levels of adrenaline.

Orange: Good for treating eczema, lack of energy, renal problems, bronchitis, and asthma. Orange is extremely effective in the treatment of throat and respiratory problems, and it also can help to alleviate the discomfort of influenza, colds, and stomach problems. It encourages the assimilation of vitamin C in the body, aiding recovery from illness. When combined with blue, orange vibrations become even more powerful in the treatment of stomach and bowel cancer.

Yellow: The vibrations of yellow are useful in the treatment of constipation, gallbladder problems, and lack of energy. The tonal effects of yellow stimulate the appetite and encourage nervous stability. When combined in treatments with blue, it produces a washing or cleansing effect over the body and serves as a tonic to a depleted nervous system. The tonal effects of yellow also aid the memory when studying for exams. The combination of yellow, orange, and green has the effect of stimulating all the major organs of the body, speeding recovery after surgery.

Green: Use for heart and lung problems, nervous disorders, depression, and holistic treatment. The tonal effects of green encourage harmony and balance and calmness to an anxious mind. Green also encourages decisive thinking and a clear mind. The tonal effects of green may be integrated with blue or indigo in the treatment of cancer and many other diseases. Green may be effectively combined with any color to form a powerful holistic healing agent. Green also produces a stabilizing effect on the body, encouraging equilibrium on all levels of consciousness.

Blue: Good for painful and inflammatory conditions, anxiety, and depression. Blue will also help to reduce a high temperature. Its tonal effects may be used in the treatment of pneumonia and other bronchial conditions. The vibrations of blue encourage harmony and balance and may be used for all types of neurological and psychological disorders. Overall, blue is calming to an anxious or stressed mind. As the tonal effects of blue are multidimensional, it may be integrated into a treatment with any of the six other colors.

Indigo: The tonal effects of indigo will help when poor concentration is causing problems. It is also effective in the treatment of a poor memory, depression, or grief. The healing effects of indigo cover a wide spectrum of ailments, ranging from dermatological problems such as psoriasis and eczema to the more serious conditions affecting the major organs of the body. Indigo also has a soothing effect on taut nerves and calms a restless mind.

Violet: This is the highest color in the visible spectrum and may be combined with any other color. Violet and its varying shades and degrees are effective in the treatment of all painful and inflammatory conditions and all serious blood conditions. Violet also produces a holistic effect upon the person and is an extremely powerful tonic. Because its vibratory tones are so powerful, exposure to it should be kept to a minimum, as oversaturation of violet may cause fatigue or even irritation.

Remember, the above suggestions are merely guidelines to help you when ascertaining what colors to use when treating the listed conditions. I would suggest that you be guided by your intuition and maybe combine the colors I have suggested with colors you think would be beneficial to whomever you are treating.

The vibratory tones of color have an extremely remarkable effect on the nadis and help in the absorption of prana. The curative effects of this process occur within a matter of hours, depending on the severity of the condition.

Although a chrome therapy light box (if you have one) may be used to bathe you with the appropriate colors in the actual process of infusing your body with the vibratory color tones you lack, I have a found a much simpler and just as effective way is to use colored light bulbs in a table lamp. Ten to fifteen minutes' exposure to each color will suffice—longer if you feel comfortable. Some colors are more intense than others and saturate the subtle anatomy much quicker. However, if you feel quite relaxed sitting for longer than I have suggested under a red light, for example, then do so. This would be a good indication that your body needs the tonal rays of that particular color. Besides, color healing is not in any way harmful, and it will rejuvenate your own personal energies.

NADI TECHNIQUE 20: *Visualizing Color*

Prana is easily influenced by color, and when integrated into the nadi technique of healing, it becomes an extremely efficient way of restoring the body's own natural resources of the vital force. Of course, the previous technique is only one of many ways in which prana can be used in the nadi technique process of healing; there are more practical methods that require the practitioner's mental interaction.

Prana also responds to the imagination and can easily be mentally infused with color vibrations before being directed into your body. With your fingertips placed gently on your solar plexus, breathe rhythmically for a few moments to increase the inflowing prana.

Prana can be inhaled and directed to any particular part of your own body where healing is needed. Simply visualize the streams of prana as intense white light flowing into your solar plexus with the incoming breath, and when your breath is complete, hold it while you transfer your fingertips to the top of your head, and then breathe the intense white light out through your fingertips, seeing it mentally streaming into your head. It is important to maintain the imagery; do not allow your mind to drift even for a moment from the visualization. Mental interaction is an integral part of this nadi technique, therefore visualization is vitally important and should be maintained constantly throughout the self-healing treatment.

Repeat the process several times and then relax with your hands resting lightly on your lap and your eyes closed.

As always, at the conclusion of the treatment, pour water backward and forward from one glass to another until it sparkles and comes alive before it is consumed.

Moving Prana for the Benefit of Others

The need to heal is deeply woven into our biological makeup and is an integral part of our natural instinctive nature. A mother comforts her child when the child has fallen, and will lovingly soothe away the discomfort by gently rubbing the painful knee. Within moments the child recovers and carries on playing, without giving any more thought to the bruised knee. A caring nurse will gently reassure the sick patient with a warm hand and softly spoken words.

We've all experienced healing at some time in our lives, whether it has been in our mother's loving arms or from the kind words of a teacher at school. But you must have noticed that not all people have this ability and that a minority exude anything but healing. In fact, some people appear cold and unfriendly, and others send out strong signals warning us not to come too close, perhaps because they are afraid to show any signs of warmth or love. However, some individuals are so gentle and loving that it's always a pleasure to meet them and stop for a little chat.

You may have on the odd occasion been feeling a little miserable and under the weather when you bumped into the elderly lady across the street. She always seems to be smiling and sufficiently astute to see that all is not well with you. A few moments spent in the old lady's company is all that is required to put the smile back on your face and a spring in your step. What is it about such people who seem to possess that certain something that they always unconsciously pass on to others? Whatever it is, it is what makes a nurse caring and good at her job and a doctor sufficiently observant to know you are unwell without you having to tell him what symptoms you are experiencing.

Without this certain something, healing cannot transpire between the healer and the patient. Simply thinking that you've got what it takes to be a healer when you have not is just being self-deluded and can very often do more harm than good, simply by filling a sick person with false hope. I have seen this happen so many times in the field of healing. Today it is far too easy for someone to embark upon the path of healing and to become a member of some healing organization. After serving the required probationary period, a certificate is awarded to endorse that the person is a qualified healer. Perhaps it's not always as easy as that, but I am sure you get the gist of what I am saying.

We have already established that if the mind is capable of worrying you into an early grave, then it is equally as capable of encouraging the health to improve as well as increasing your longevity. Transcendental healing is the ability to focus the attention on an individual whose body lacks vitality and balance, with the sole intention of restoring their equilibrium.

Once you begin using the nadi technique of transcendental healing, you can usually very quickly tell when a person is out of sorts or generally under the weather. You should notice an overwhelming dullness and lack of luster in their personal energy, which is usually a good indication that their body is lacking in vitality. Provided there is no serious underlying cause for the apparent lack of zest and vitality, the condition can be quickly remedied. The same process applies when treating yourself. There are two ways of encouraging an increase in the levels of vitality: one with the person's cooperation, and the other, remotely. Either treatment requires the person's permission. At least, before beginning the treatment, mentally request this, perhaps in the silence. Let's take a look at the first method.

NADI TECHNIQUE 21:
Pranic Movement for Another With Cooperation

Anyone can perform this treatment. Make certain the person is seated comfortably on a straight-backed chair with their eyes closed.

Stand behind them with your hands resting lightly on their shoulders, quietly attuning your mind to them.

Ask them to breathe rhythmically, making certain that the inhalations and exhalations are evenly spaced, while you follow the same process, synchronizing your breathing with theirs as best as you can. This encourages the precipitation of prana in their body as well as your own.

Remove your hands and shake them as vigorously as you can until they tingle and feel alive with vitality. The shaking process stimulates the nerves and nadis in your hands and encourages the facilitation of prana in preparation for the treatment.

Extend the index finger of both hands, securing the other fingers with your thumbs, and gently touch the mastoid bone behind each of the person's ears with the tip of your index fingers.

Holding them in this position, breathe in slowly and deeply, and as you do so, pull back the thumb of each hand as though pulling back the hammer on a handgun while imagining streams of intense white light being drawn through your extended fingers. When this procedure is complete, hold your breath for the count of three before slowly breathing out, closing your thumbs once again, and visualizing streams of white light pouring into the person's head.

Repeat this procedure several times before relaxing, with your hands on the person's shoulders. Remain in this position, concluding the treatment with some rhythmic breathing.

As on the conclusion of all such treatments, pour a glass of water backward and forward from one tumbler to another until it sparkles and comes alive, and then give it to the patient to drink. This ensures that the movement of prana is encouraged to circulate through the nadis.

NADI TECHNIQUE 22:
Pranic Movement for Another Without Cooperation

There are specific trigger or power points that are effective in the process of remote healing, and when these are combined with a focused mind, they are extremely effective. Although technically it is what some would term "distance healing," this method requires a little more technique to initiate.

These particular nadi finger positions are more effective when mentally programmed in preparation for the administration of healing. This is easily initiated by sitting quietly and going through each position (which will soon be discussed) while mentally saying what you intend using them for. This eventually empowers each finger position so that when they are used in the healing process, there is absolutely no need to think of anything other than the person to whom the healing force is being directed. The finger positions may also be used with some extremely effective results on yourself. In some of the nadi technique's healing methods, the mind is the common denominator, and the simplest of movements are the most effective. The more the finger positions are used, the stronger and more effective they become.

By using the thumb as a conduit for the conveyance of energy, it is possible to program each finger with a specific intention and focus, and simply by connecting the thumb with the selected finger, the energy is released. For an example, you may use the little finger to promote relaxation, so simply touching the thumb with the little finger will instantly encourage relaxation and calm. You may want to use the index finger to help you take control of a stressful situation; once the finger has been programmed for this, the appropriate energies will instantly be released to help you take control.

You might look upon finger positions as sort of mnemonics in memory training; the principle is the same and the results just as effective. When you've programmed these positions, you can move on to offering remote healing.

For the process of sending healing remotely, as explained previously, some time should be spent beforehand mentally programming and creating a connection between the middle fingers and the thumbs of both hands, with the sole intention of mentally energizing the fingers to transmit healing. It requires little effort and is so simple.

Sit on a straight-backed chair, maintaining an erect posture. Breathe rhythmically, with your eyes closed, and in your mind slowly establish an image of the person to whom the healing is to be directed. Should it be for yourself, then simply focus your attention on yourself.

Press the middle finger of each hand gently against the thumb at the same time as maintaining a clear image of the person (or yourself) in your mind.

Maintain this position for thirty seconds, slowly increasing the pressure of your middle fingers against your thumbs and maintaining this until both hands feel quite rigid. This is an indication that the levels of prana are building up and are nearly ready to be released.

Still with the image of the person clearly in your mind, release the middle fingers of both hands and now secure the ring fingers gently in place against the thumbs. Maintain this for a further thirty seconds, gradually increasing the pressure until the hands feel rigid, and then relax.

Although slight variations on the more traditional finger positions, in Eastern practices they are known as mudras and are usually engaged in meditation with specific symbolic meaning. They are also regarded as hand disciplines for the sole purpose of contemplation and meditation.

Many people take their own bodies for granted, with the mistaken belief that whatever befalls it is meant to be. Although we genetically inherit both weaknesses and strengths from our parents, the quality of our health can be enhanced through practices such as these, which fine-tune the subtle energy system so that it performs more efficiently.

4

Fine-Tuning
the Energy Body

Earlier we touched on the importance of music in meditation. Previously we examined how humans are far more than a biological unit comprised of a collection of cells and that the human organism is an electromagnetic unit of incredible power that exists within its own spectrum of light and color. We are, to all intents and purposes, human rainbows—electromagnetically charged and infused with a dynamic cosmic force. We are much more powerful than we realize, and the colors that surround us collectively emit a musical tone. Although inaudible to the human ear, this tone is so powerful that it produces a resonance with the surrounding atmosphere as well as with all those with whom we come into contact.

Usually as a consequence of stress, poor diet, or even wrong thinking, this musical tone sometimes changes pitch. Once our frequency alters, so too does the polarity of our life, very often causing us to be attracted to unsuitable situations and circumstances as well as encouraging us to act impulsively and even to make wrong decisions. This may be equated with a radio whose tuning dial has moved between stations, creating a cacophony of distorted sounds consisting of white noise and indistinct voices. Although a simple analogy, it explains perfectly well the nature of human frequency and range and how our minds are affected when we are out of tune, so to speak, with the universe.

I am not talking here just about the human aura, although this must be included in our consideration of human range and frequency. Although a metaphysical phenomenon, the aura can also be scientifically calculated as a precise measure of human consciousness as well as a sophisticated radar and homing device. Before anything can be achieved, you must first of all ascertain whether or not your personal frequency has altered at all. This is done by answering some simple questions, the first being from a psychological perspective and the second from a transcendental metaphysical perspective.

First of all, from the psychological perspective:

- How have the last couple of years been for you?
- Have you encountered any insurmountable difficulties?
- Have you been prone to minor health problems?

Now from a transcendental metaphysical perspective:

- Have you noticed that your dreams have recently become more lucid?
- Are you occasionally overwhelmed with morbid thoughts, even when you feel quite happy?
- Do you go through periods when you feel totally insecure?

Although the majority of us have experienced all of the above at some time or another, if you answer yes to all of the questions, then we must assume that your frequency has altered. In order to come back into a harmonious state, follow these techniques.

NADI TECHNIQUE 23: *Ascertaining Your Color Range*

If you are already stressed, then you will most probably have some difficulty getting a quiet moment to yourself. Should that be the case, you must set about creating a sacred space. This can be anywhere you choose—a quiet corner of the house, perhaps, that says to the family *leave me alone!* Perhaps even a peaceful corner of the garden (weather permitting) where you can be alone with your thoughts. Wherever you choose to create your sacred space, make it your own private sanctuary and a place to which you can withdraw whenever you feel a need.

It is important that you instill into your mind that while you are in your sacred space, nothing can touch you. Once this has been encoded into your thinking processes, you can always retreat there whenever you feel stressed or emotionally threatened in anyway whatsoever.

Before you begin, you will need a notebook to keep a record of the things that occur.

Sit quietly with your eyes closed and your hands resting lightly on your lap. Mentally scan your body, beginning with your head and then slowly working your way down to your toes, seeing your body as the sequential colors of the spectrum.

Next, take your left wrist in your right hand and span it, securely closing your thumb and middle finger together, until you can feel the throb of a pulse anywhere in either your fingers or hand. What is the first color that comes into your mind? Take time out to write this down.

Now, in the same way as previously shown, take your right wrist in your left hand and span this securely with your middle finger and thumb, closing them together until you can feel the throb of a pulse anywhere. What color comes into your mind? Write this down.

Now rest the back of your left hand gently in the palm of your right hand, ensuring that the left palm is facing upwards, with the fingers of both hands fully extended. Make a mental note of the color that now comes into your mind, and then write this down. You may not see a color straightaway, so wait a few moments until you do.

Now do the same with the back of your right hand resting lightly in your left palm, again with your right palm facing upwards and the fingers of both hands fully extended. What color comes into your mind? Write it down.

Before moving on to the next part, spend a few moments relaxing and breathing rhythmically, as usual making certain that the inhalations and exhalations are evenly spaced.

Take a break for a few moments to consider the colors you have already written down. Because you may already be familiar with the meanings of color, particularly in relation to the aura, before moving on we need to first of all eliminate any possibility that you may have selected the colors purposely and did not allow them to come into your mind of their own accord. The previous exercises need to be repeated several times, ensuring that there is no conscious involvement in the way the colors are produced. The only way this can be successfully achieved is for you to relax and just allow the colors to appear in your consciousness.

NADI TECHNIQUE 24: *Ascertaining Your Key of Life*

Your "Key of Life" is a culmination of your life energies, which create a musical resonance with the surrounding environment as well as with the universe. There's nothing at all complicated in it. It's simply a matter of feeling "in tune" with everything else. Your Key of Life is an important part of what makes you tick and an integral part of what keeps you healthy and happy. Although somewhat of a cliché, when your body is perfectly tuned, you are in harmony with the universe. And so, for the purpose of this procedure, look upon yourself as a sequence of colorful musical tones perfectly in tune.

First of all, take a look at the colors' musical value below. This should give you a better idea what we are endeavoring to achieve.

COLOR	MUSICAL RESONANCE	CHAKRA
Red	C	Base of the Spine
Orange	D	Sacral
Yellow	E	Solar Plexus
Green	F	Heart
Blue	G	Throat
Indigo	A	Brow
Violet	B	Crown

In music there are two notes that technically do not have a sharp: E and B. When E is raised a semitone it becomes F, and when B is raised a semitone it becomes C, both completely changing key. If your Key of Life turns out to be either of these notes, then you can rest assured that you have always been highly sensitive. People who resonate with the musical keys of E or B are usually extremely gifted either creatively or spiritually, and if not consistently maintained, you will always feel somewhat out of place in the scheme of things—or, to put it another way, out of tune with everything else. However, balance may be achieved in various ways.

If the colors produced in the exercises are consistently the same each time, then you can safely assume that these are your strongest and most vibrant energies, and it will then be a good indication as to what is either wrong or right about the color arrangements of your personal energy field. Although in the process we consider the whole musical/color spectrum, we are really only concerned with four notes in these procedures, as these represent the harmonics of the mind and will help you in determining your Key of Life. The important notes in this process are E, F, B, and C, and these resonate to the colors yellow, green, violet, and red. These colors, in fact, predominate the subtle vibratory structure of the human organism. Notes F and C are distortions of E and B and are indicative of complete discord, at least where the subtle anatomy is concerned. If it transpires that you resonate with the keys of F or C, then only consistent results will positively confirm whether or not you have moved from either E or B or whether F or C has always been your natural key.

Let us take a look at the colors you gleaned from the clasping the wrist procedure. The left wrist is directly connected to a major nadi known as ida. This nadi is referred to as the female channel, and in yoga it is represented by the symbol of the moon. The right wrist is connected to pingala nadi and is referred to as the male channel; in yoga it is symbolically represented by the sun. Ideally, for a female the colors gleaned from the wrist procedure should be green and blue (musical resonance F and G) and for a male red and orange (musical resonance C and D).

For a female, the left hand on the right hand and right hand on the left hand should ideally produce the colors blue and indigo respectively (musical resonance G and A), and for a male orange and yellow respectively (musical resonance D and E), although these are only guidelines and may vary from person to person. Not only will this procedure help to polarize the chakra system, but it will also seal any fragmentations that may have occurred in your aura. Apart from these two extremely important procedures, determining what color and key you are brings about a complete transformation of the polarity of your life, encouraging a more positive outlook and improving overall health in the long term.

Should your colors not be as clear or as intense as they should be, a simple mental process will give them more clarity and make them more refined.

Simply imagine yourself bathed in a beautiful wash of blue light. Hold it for a few seconds before changing the blue light into a red light. Maintain this imagery for a few seconds further before changing it into a bright yellow light, then turn the yellow light into a golden light. Hold this for a few seconds further, and then dissolve it all from your mind and relax.

To achieve maximum results, the exercise should be practiced every day for at least a week. This mental process produces a washing or cleansing effect on the subtle energies of the aura, thus encouraging consistency and balance. As always, at the conclusion of the exercise, drink a glass of charged water.

For this next experiment, you will need to enlist the help of a sympathetic friend, someone who fully understands what you are endeavoring to achieve.

You will also require four metal discs approximately 2.5 centimeters in diameter and a pendulum, preferably crystal. The metal discs serve as conduits and help to neutralize the subtle energies in the chakras you are dowsing, and the magnets help to magnetize and polarize them, encouraging more consistent activity in each one. You will need to be in a horizontal position, preferably on the floor, with a cushion to support your head.

The four metal discs should be placed precisely on the chakra corresponding with the colors gleaned during the previous experiment.

Your friend should commence dowsing these points sequentially, making a note of the way in which the pendulum rotates, as this will tell you which is the strongest point. For example, should three of the dowsed metal discs cause a clockwise motion in the pendulum, then the one with the counterclockwise movement possesses the strongest musical resonance and represents your Key of Life. To ensure that accurate results have been achieved, repeat the process several times.

It may well be that the results produced by the dowsing are inconsistent and keep changing. If this is the case, what you should be looking for is the point with the strongest and most energetic movement.

Even when you are satisfied that you have the final accurate conclusion and you've got your personal key, it will occasionally change anyway depending on what is occurring in your life. But as long as you continue with the exercise, your Key of Life will always normalize itself.

NADI TECHNIQUE 25:
Magnetic Treatment for Maintaining Color Resonance

Although color resonance can be maintained through visualization, exerting mental control over the subtle energies in this way is unreliable, in my experience, and produces results that are very rarely permanent. Even though the procedures I have given are extremely effective, an occasional overhaul to maintain balance should be carried out, particularly when things are not going so well in your life. The nadi technique addresses subtle energy problems directly, and with the use of seven metal magnets the chakras can be effectively realigned, thus increasing the polarity of each one. Normalizing the chakras in this way also produces a positive effect on the color resonance and helps to normalize the frequency and range of the overall color arrangements of the subtle anatomy.

Metal magnets come in different strengths, and the more powerful the magnet, the stronger the effect on the subtle anatomy. Therefore it would be advisable to use magnets of medium strength. Besides, the more powerful magnets are extremely difficult to use. Magnets of all strengths can be obtained online at e-magnetsuk.com (look for the therapy magnets).

Cautionary note: Do not use magnets on or near anyone who is fitted with a heart pacemaker.

Lie on the floor with a cushion to support your head, and then position the magnets more or less in line with each chakra.

As it would be difficult to place a magnet on the crown of the head, position one as far back on the forehead as possible, securing it in the hairline if necessary.

Leave the magnets in their respective positions for five minutes and then remove them. Your friend should dowse each chakra point to establish the degree of movement in each one. Write these results down. The magnets should then be returned to their respective positions and allowed to remain there for a further five minutes.

After the magnets have been removed, the chakra points should be dowsed again and a note made of any changes in their movement.

This procedure should be repeated until the rotation of the pendulum at each point produces consistent results, as this will show their correct polarity.

To make sure color resonance has successfully been stabilized, place the four metal discs (without the magnets) on the chakras that correspond with the four colors you originally gleaned from the initial procedures, and allow your friend to dowse these to establish in which direction they are rotating.

This procedure should be performed four times. If the results are consistent, you've successfully fine-tuned your energy body. To ensure that the color resonance has been permanently normalized, it is a good idea for the procedure to be repeated at least once a month.

NADI TECHNIQUE 26:
Maintenance of Magnetic Resonance

If you aren't able to work with a partner to regularly maintain chakra activity and encourage a consistent flow of energy through the nadis, magnetic resonance can be effectively used in the following way.

Sit comfortably on a straight-backed chair. Hold a magnet in each hand. Make sure that your chest, neck, and head are in as straight a line as possible, with the shoulders thrown slightly back. Although this treatment is similar to the one shown earlier using clear quartz crystals, the use of magnets is much more powerful and produces amazing results.

Place one hand (holding a magnet) on top of your head, and place the other hand (holding a magnet) at the lowest part of your back. Allow the hands to remain in that position until you feel a temperature change in one or both hands.

Now, reverse the hand positions by placing the one on your head at the base of your spine and moving the one at the base of your spine to the top of your head.

Repeat this process for five to ten minutes, and then relax, with your hands on your lap (with the magnets resting on the upward-facing palms) and your eyes closed.

Although visualization is not absolutely essential, it does help with the process of energy circulation through the intricate network of nadis. See the energy as intense white light streaming down one channel from the head to the base of the spine, and then up the other channel toward the head. Be consistent with the imagery, maintaining the flow of energy backward and forward in one constant stream. It also helps if you feel the force as well as see it as it passes along the nadis.

Alternating the position of the hands helps to maintain activity in the two major nadis, ida and pingala, thus encouraging balance and equilibrium throughout the subtle anatomy.

Vibration and Chanting

Music is encoded into our biological makeup, making us who and what we are. Music most certainly affects the mind to such an extent as to evoke feeling and thoughts of our past lives. I'm sure everyone will agree that music of any kind is important to us. It lifts our spirits when we are sad or feeling depressed, and certain pieces of music can even encourage feelings of melancholy and nostalgia, causing us to reflect upon the past. The vibration of sound affects all the cells of the body, encouraging us back to health when we are under the weather, and it can even stimulate our mental processes when we are engaged in a difficult task. In recent years psychologists have recommended a background of music to encourage workers' performance in the workplace. It certainly works on all levels of consciousness, but on a more subtle level music has a remarkable effect upon the nadis and encourages the precipitation of prana through the intricate network of channels.

But what about chanting to encourage the movement of energy, with the sole intention of stimulating the body, mind, and spirit? Chanting can take many different forms, from the more traditional mantras such as *Om* or *Aum* to the more involved mantra of *Om mani padme hum*, the "jewel in the lotus" of mantras. In fact, chanted in a specific way, they can quite easily produce a resonance with the mind and encourage balance in the body.

From time immemorial, man has used chanting in one form or another to attain higher states of consciousness. From the repetitive chanting of the Tibetan monks to the scrying techniques of the yogic masters, various mental exercises have always been employed as safe ways of attaining heightened states of awareness. Chanting is often integrated into meditation to attain *samadhi*, a state of consciousness that lies beyond waking, dreaming, and deep sleep and in which all mental activity ceases. This state of consciousness is frequently referred to as "one-pointedness of mind," a phrase which is completely misleading, as this would suggest that samadhi is purely a state of concentration on one point. Samadhi is not achieved through straining concentration on one point, nor is it achieved through the mind's focus on one point to another; it requires total absorption and can take many years of experience to achieve. The literal meaning of samadhi is "establish" or "make firm." Samadhi is a total absorption in meditation (*dhyana*), the result of which is union with God or the Absolute.

Meditation is regarded as being the tool of all great minds, and in some ways it is viewed as the highest form of prayer. Reciting a special word with meaning—a mantra—is an extremely effective way of focusing the attention with the sole object of altering the frequency of the mind and raising the consciousness. Although the mantra may really be any word of your choice, there are a few mantras that bear great spiritual significance in the process of meditation.

Let us take, for an example, *Om mani padme hum* and how this can be effectively used to increase the vibratory levels of the mind, body, and spirit.

NADI TECHNIQUE 27: *Om Mani Padme Hum*

As always, sit comfortably, with your back straight, your eyes closed, and your hands resting lightly on your lap. Breathe rhythmically for a few minutes, ensuring that the inhalations and exhalations are evenly spaced.

When the mind is quiet and you feel quite relaxed, begin chanting the whole mantra, *Om mani padme hum*, on the exhalation of breath, suspending it very briefly while you inhale a complete breath, and then commencing the chanting once again on the exhalation.

Repeat this process for at least ten minutes (longer if comfortable). You should feel a sense of invigoration gradually passing through the brain.

When the ten minutes have elapsed, suspend the chanting for a further two minutes and sit quietly, imbibing the pleasant sensation as it washes over you. You may feel as though every nerve, tissue, and cell in your body is buzzing as a feeling of calm overwhelms you.

This time, commence chanting *Om mani padme hum* and at the same time create in your mind's eye the image of a clear pond, in the center of which there is a beautiful lotus flower. Still chanting *Om mani padme hum*, see a faceted jewel resting in the center of the lotus, glistening in the bright sunlight.

Continue the chanting while focusing your attention on the picture of the lotus flower and the jewel. Be totally mindful of what you are chanting; at the same time, be conscious of your breathing, and with each exhalation infuse the imagery with brightness and clarity.

Continue the chanting and visualization for as long as you feel comfortable. When you are ready, allow the chanting to fade into nothingness and your image of the lotus to gradually fade away. Sit quietly for a few minutes longer, again imbibing the energy created during the process. When you feel that it has reached its conclusion, inhale a complete breath and then, when you exhale, dissolve it all from your mind and open your eyes.

The majority of people have little or no problem with the actual chanting, but integrating the visualization into the process occasionally presents a problem. You will need to persevere and practice as much as you can before the desired results are achieved. It may well be that you will have no problem combining the two, in which case it should be used at least once a day—time permitting, of course.

NADI TECHNIQUE 28: *Chanting for Each Chakra*

Meditation, visualization, and chanting mantras form an integral part of the nadi technique and the whole process of controlling energy in the subtle channels, with the sole intention of encouraging harmony and balance as well as heightening the awareness. This can effectively be achieved with the nadi technique, which addresses human disharmony on all levels. Because the chakra system is an integral part of human consciousness and its spiritual development, the individual chakras can also be effectively influenced by certain sounds.

Each chakra is not only symbolically represented by a geometric shape or design called a yantra, but the release of the chakra's inherent qualities may also be encouraged by the chanting of *bija* mantras, specific sounds designed to affect the chakras. The bija mantras produce positive effects upon each individual chakra and the minute subtle channels. Once the chanting of the bija mantras has been successfully achieved, activation of the individual centers occurs and the flow of energy along the nadis is encouraged. However, in order for the maximum results to be achieved, such a release can only be brought about gradually. Incidentally, the word *bija* means semen, seed, or center, the full release of the very center of the chakra.

Chanting the bija mantras produces a stimulating effect upon all the glands of the body and also helps to keep the channels clear. Apart from that, chanting also produces an invigorating effect upon the brain and feelings of euphoria similar to those experienced after a rigorous exercise regime.

Although single bija mantras may be used for the purpose of focusing on one specific chakra, to achieve maximum results and encourage an evenly balanced and harmonious subtle energy system, the bija mantras should be chanted in sequential order, beginning with the base chakra and the word *Lam*.

Before you begin the process of chanting, it is a good idea to spend a few minutes learning the words by rote. Here is a list of the bija mantras and their corresponding chakras:

CHAKRA	BIJA MANTRA
Base	Lam
Sacral	Vam
Solar Plexus	Ram
Heart	Yam
Throat	Ham
Brow	Ksham (silent K)
Crown	Om

Sit comfortably with your eyes closed, ensuring that your chest, neck, and head are in as straight a line as possible, with your shoulders thrown slightly back and your hands resting lightly on your lap.

Inhale a complete breath, and on the exhalation begin chanting the words *Lam, Vam, Ram, Yam, Ham, Ksham, Om*—inhale—*Lam, Vam, Ram, Yam, Ham, Ksham, Om*—inhale—and so on, in quick succession.

Repeat the chanting for at least ten minutes, pausing only for the inhalation. When the ten minutes of chanting has elapsed, continue to chant the words while clapping your hands simultaneously with each intonation. The clapping also stimulates the nadis and precipitates prana through the channels.

Continue the clapping and chanting for a further five minutes, then sit quietly still, with your eyes closed and your hands placed gently on your solar plexus. Feel your whole body almost buzzing and imbibe the energy that has been created during the chanting. Initially you may find the experience quite unpleasant, but if you persist it will become extremely invigorating. In fact, the effects of this sort of chanting are quite holistic and very often last throughout the day.

To experience maximum results from the chanting, it is always best to ensure that you have nothing whatsoever to do during the day that is in any way taxing. Although a little more difficult, the chanting may be done mentally if you prefer, allowing the words to be repeated silently in sequential order. Once mastered, mental chanting is probably far more effective than chanting out loud.

Practiced daily chanting helps to energize the nervous system and helps to maintain the flow of prana through the subtle channels. For the person who enjoys chanting, this is ideal when you are feeling lethargic and lacking in mental stamina, and it is also an effective treatment for anyone recovering from nervous exhaustion. Chanting bija mantras is also an extremely effective discipline to encourage a more efficient mind and may be used to complement meditation. The benefits of this are long lasting and also encourage the equilibrium of body, mind, and spirit.

NADI TECHNIQUE 29:
Chanting for Specific Physical Intent

The following sounds are recognized by many practitioners of sound and vocal therapy as producing powerful effects upon the glands and organs of the body. More than this, though, when integrated into the nadi technique, they encourage movement of energy in the nadis and also in the chakras corresponding with the glands that the sounds affect. Of course, as with all systems of chanting, words may be changed or modified to suit you. In her book *Forever Young, Forever Healthy*, yoga teacher Indra Devi explains how chanting words such as the following is good for the health by toning all the major glands of the body.

Mmee: This produces an amazing effect upon the pituitary and pineal glands, and encourages an increase in the electromagnetic waves emanating from the pineal gland. To use the mantra, inhale a complete breath, then chant the word until all the breath has been fully exhaled. Repeat the process four times before moving on to the next.

Ea: Ea should be sounded as in the word *feather*. This mantra affects the throat area and particularly the thyroid. As previously explained, inhale a complete breath, then sound the word until all the breath has been fully expelled. Repeat this four times before moving on to the next sound.

Aaa: Aaa should be sounded like the word *arm*, following the same procedure as previously shown. This particular mantra affects the upper respiratory area of the body.

Ou-o: Ou-o should be sounded as in the word *water*, with the same procedure given in the previous mantras. The vibrations with this sound affect the middle area of the chest.

Ooo: Ooo should be sounded like the word *home*, again with the same breathing procedure as previously shown. This word has a remarkable effect upon the heart, stomach, liver, and lower part of the lungs.

Eur: Eur should be sounded as in the French word *fleur* and chanted in the same way as the previous words. The vibratory sounds of this word affect the diaphragm and surrounding area.

U-ee: U-ee should be sounded as in "you-ee" and allowed to resonate until the breath has been fully expelled. The vibratory sounds of this word affect the gonads of the male and the female reproductive systems.

Mmmmmm-Po-Mmmmmm: According to Indra Devi and Yogi Ramacharaka, this is an excellent mantra for stimulating the heart as well as the corresponding chakra. As this mantra vibrates the heart area, it would be advisable to use this only once a day. In fact, if there is a history of weakness in this area, the practitioner should begin by strengthening the heart first of all with a much shorter version: *Mmm-Po-Mmm,* followed by *Paaaaeeeeee* in one long breath. Remember not to strain or make it a labor, as this merely defeats the whole object of the exercise.

A little experimentation may well help you to find other more suitable mantras that stimulate the different organs of the body. If they produce more effective results, then by all means use them. Combinations of mantras may be integrated into your daily program. As long as they stimulate you and do not make you feel exhausted, then you can rest assured that they are working for you.

Magnetic Therapy

When magnetic therapy is integrated into the nadi technique, it becomes an extremely powerful healing tool. The interaction between magnetism and prana creates an incredible force through the individual energy channels of the subtle anatomy.

Before we move any further, it is necessary to give you an understanding of exactly what magnetic therapy is and how it can produce some remarkable biological effects. As the human aura is a vaporous mass of electromagnetic particles, magnetic treatment encourages its bioluminescence to be consistently brighter, with a more vibrant overall appearance. In the presence of someone who has been treated with magnetism, a sick person usually feels overwhelmed and invigorated. The advantages of magnetism are quite extensive, and frequent treatments holistically affect the health—and that includes promoting harmony and equilibrium throughout the entire subtle anatomy.

Magnetic therapy involves the transmission of electromagnetic impulses that affect the overall resonance of an individual's personal energy field. The metal magnets augment the individual's aura, strengthening it and ultimately sealing any leakages or fragmentations that lead to poor health and disease in the long term. Not to be confused with prana, which some people store in their bodies in large amounts, human magnetism has been used through antiquity as a means of healing a diseased body.

In his book *Science of Breath*, Yogi Ramacharaka states that in the seventeenth century, when the chemist and physician Van Helmont was writing, a Scotsman by the name of Maxwell was practicing and teaching the art of magnetic healing. Although this was looked upon with some disdain by the church, Maxwell's belief in an all-pervading vital spirit that could be tapped for healing the sick caught the imagination of his numerous devotees.

Also according to Ramacharaka's *Science of Breath,* a similar idea became popular in 1734 when a priest by the name of Father Hehl propagated the idea of a "universal fluid" that could be used to cure all manner of illnesses. Needless to say, Father Hehl was branded a heretic and driven from the church.

At the end of the eighteenth century, Friedrich Anton Mesmer (the innovator of mesmerism, the forerunner to hypnotism) taught the radical and unconventional theory of animal magnetism. Initially, Mesmer was held in high esteem in Vienna and Paris, and was looked upon as a sort of guru of his day. The Prussian government established a hospital devoted to the application of magnetic healing, and such was the interest in the subject that strict laws were introduced by various continental governments to prevent anyone outside the medical profession from using magnetic treatments. Nonetheless, Mesmer and his ideas fell into disfavor, and some of his followers seized the opportunity to exploit the knowledge they had obtained from him, thus prostituting what they had learned. However, their interpretation of his teachings did give birth to new schools of thought centered primarily around the transference of magnetic energy.

In the mid-nineteenth century, treating the body with metal magnets became quite fashionable and was hailed as a sort of miracle cure for all maladies. The treatment was also seen as a pick-me-up for those recovering from consumption and other health conditions. Although many medical practitioners were skeptical about these claims, the majority agreed that magnetic treatments did successfully ease painful and inflammatory conditions as well as revitalize the blood when a person suffered from anemia.

Metal magnets combined with copper discs appear to produce amazing effects on the body's energy resources and have been known not only to alleviate painful conditions but to cure them altogether. Magnetic and copper treatments also work at a more subtle level by encouraging a breakdown of energy crystallization in the nadis that permeate the subtle anatomy.

The aura may also be looked upon as a sort of blueprint of the individual it represents; it contains all relevant data about the person's psychological, spiritual, and physical makeup. In other words, everything you need to know about a person is contained in the electromagnetic energy field and may be accessed at any time. To reiterate what I have said earlier, disease is seen in the aura a considerable time before it becomes apparent in

FINE-TUNING THE ENERGY BODY

the physical body, and so treating it with magnetic therapy helps greatly with the healing process.

Metal magnets not only encourage a washing effect on the human aura, but they also help to polarize it and seal any leakages or fragmentations. Because the aura extends some distance from the body, it is not absolutely necessary to actually make physical contact with the person, although this does seem to be more effective. The following section is another example of how magnetic treatment should be implemented.

NADI TECHNIQUE 30:
Magnetic Healing for Aura Polarization

For this particular magnetic treatment, you will only require two metal magnets of a fairly powerful strength that are large enough to hold comfortably in your hands. (The strength of magnets varies; a full list of magnets and their strength can be obtained at http://e-magnetsuk.com/magnets/magnet_therapy .aspx.)

Take a magnet in each hand and, while seated, begin by holding them above your head about 5 to 6 cm from the head and approximately 7 to 8 cm from each other.

Begin the treatment by slowly moving the magnets in opposite directions around the sides of your body, working downwards and shaking your hands slightly as you move them.

Take time with the treatment. When you have reached the hip area, follow the same route back up to the top of the head. Repeat this process three or four times.

Following the same procedure as before, this time move one magnet down your back (as best as you can) and one down the front, again taking time with the treatment.

Remember, although you are treating the subtle energies of the aura, you are actually using the magnetic properties of two solid objects; therefore, no visualization or mental imagery is necessary for positive results to be achieved.

Once the treatment has been concluded, a glass of charged water should be drunk to ensure that the body is fully hydrated. Note that this treatment can also be done with two people.

Because the aura has been polarized with the treatment, it is quite normal to feel lightheaded or even slightly disorientated. However, this should only last until the magnetic polarization process has taken effect, and then everything should be back to normal within five minutes. Also, before you begin the treatment, it is a good idea to spend a few minutes breathing rhythmically to ensure that you are fully relaxed. This helps the magnet treatment to be more efficient and encourages the subtle energy system to assimilate the magnetic force more effectively.

It is unnecessary to apply the treatment to the entire body, as once the magnetic waves infiltrate the upper part of the aura, the entire energy field will be affected within minutes. It is quite common to have a runny nose on the conclusion—it is one of the visible effects of magnetic resonance treatment.

5

Specific-Purpose Treatments

Integrated into the nadi technique are "power points" that may effectively be utilized to alleviate specific conditions, particularly in emergency situations, such as when in the grip of a panic attack or stricken with the excruciating pain of a migraine. These power points, as I will call them here, are simple finger positions that, when applied, lock in to a corresponding nadi to either alleviate or even cure the condition. These power points are not the same as those found in other complementary practices, as they are designed to influence the mind as well as affect the corresponding nadi to which it has been applied.

First of all, it is important to create a few simple finger positions, as in the case of the so-called mudras of Eastern meditation traditions. Creating a finger position, or posture, with a specific intention and using it over a period of time eventually encourages the release of subconscious energies to help you whenever you are in need. Here I have combined various finger positions with power points to be used for specific conditions. You can use

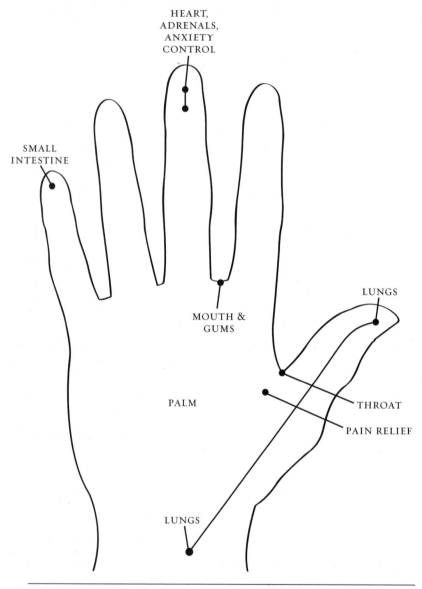

FIGURE 3: *Hand nadis*

these as an easy-to-follow reference when choosing the appropriate treatment.

Stress and Relaxation

Today there is very little doubt that stress is one of the major killers. In fact, apart from causing heart conditions and cancer, stress can also cause dermatological eruptions, anxiety neuroses, and even a complete nervous breakdown. Stress is no respecter of age; today many young people suffer from stress-related conditions.

On a more subtle level, stress also inhibits the flow of prana through the nadis, depriving the nerves of vitality and causing biological changes to occur. In fact, the biological and psychological effects of stress frequently prevent a sufferer from leading a normal, happy life. Outwardly the person may look extremely healthy, but inwardly they may be at the point of desperation.

Although somewhat exaggerated, here is an ideal way of experiencing what tension actually feels like and how its effect on the nerves, tissues, cells, and fibers can be quickly dissipated. Once you have experienced this exercise, you should then be able to quickly recognize when tension is being created in your body and be able to relieve it with some ease.

NADI TECHNIQUE 31: *Programming and Preparation*

Sitting quietly with your eyes closed, hold the middle finger gently with the other hand's fingers, focusing all your attention on this finger and visualizing energy streaming from your throat, down your arm, and along the middle finger. The visualization combined with mentally impressing the power point is paramount in the whole programming process.

Although it should be practiced at least five minutes every day for at least a week, there is no reason why it cannot be used in the meantime. The whole object of the exercise is to *believe* that it works and to look upon this power-point procedure as your instant relief from anxiety and stress. Applying pressure to the middle finger in this way affects the nadi responsible for controlling the release of adrenaline, the primary cause for the effects of panic and anxiety. It is not simply a psychological tool working at a placebo level; the more this power point is used, the more it becomes effective in calming you.

Everybody gets stressed from time to time; unfortunately, this is one of life's hard facts. Usually, though, we control our stress by using the adrenaline created by it in a constructive and positive way. In fact, the adrenaline rush is what helps us cope in stressful or threatening situations. However, occasionally stress becomes so overwhelming that it causes irrational fear—as in the case of panic attacks, which seemingly can occur at any time and for no one particular reason. Once a person has experienced a panic attack, they usually expect it to occur again, and it is this expectation that "programs" the mind into bringing the panic on exactly when it is expected. As an example: if a person has a panic attack while waiting in a queue at the bank, then they subconsciously see the bank as the primary cause for the panic attack, and so they will take every measure to avoid going to the bank.

People who have learned to panic on a regular basis will sometimes connect the panic attacks to leaving the safety of their home. Agoraphobia (the fear of open spaces) is much more common than we know, and having suffered from it myself, I know only too well how it can affect your life. Although in the extreme, agoraphobia is perhaps the very worst form of anxiety neurosis and one that can be treated with the nadi technique in exactly the same way as an ordinary panic attack. I have not only used these techniques on myself with great success, but I have also used them on many people suffering from acute panic attacks, stopping them completely. It must be said, however, that some people do need their panic attacks as a psychological security blanket. This person sometimes feels that without the regular panic attack, they would lose the attention of family and friends. In this, case a different approach is needed before the treatment begins.

Look upon your chosen power point as your personal release mechanism—something that will immediately free you from the misery of anxiety. Your belief that it will work is of paramount importance, and once you have practiced it in the comfort and safety of your own home, you will be amazed at how effectively and quickly it will work.

NADI TECHNIQUE 32: *Tense and Relax*

Sit quietly on a comfortable chair with your eyes closed and your hands resting lightly on your lap. Mentally scan your whole body, beginning with the feet, legs, abdomen, and chest, then across the shoulders and concluding with the head and face, mentally noting any tension.

Repeat the scanning process, and then relax each part of your body as you mentally look at it. Repeat this process a few times, and then just sit quietly for a little longer.

Now, very slowly, begin to make your whole body tense, beginning with your legs and moving up through the abdomen, chest muscles, and face. Make fists and squeeze as tightly as you possibly can, as though you are squeezing the juice from two oranges. Feel the tension in your fingers, hands, and arms. Screw up your face and clench your teeth. Feel your whole body quivering with tension as you make it as rigid as you possibly can. Maintain the tensing process for as long as you can possibly stand it, and then relax.

You should now be able to feel all the muscles, nerves, tissues, cells, and fibers tingling as they begin to relax. Allow your chair to support all the weight of your body as you let go.

Breathe slowly, making sure that the inhalations and exhalations are evenly spaced, and as you breathe, mentally scan your body from your feet to your head, ensuring that there is absolutely no tension whatsoever.

Remain seated and continue to relax. Maintain this feeling of calm for at least ten minutes—longer if you feel like it.

The muscle-tensing process helps to alleviate tension in the physical as well as in the subtle anatomy, and once the exercise has been concluded, prana is automatically precipitated through the nadis.

A simple nadi-tapping procedure should follow the tensing exercise. Gently tap the back of each hand with a finger, beginning by tapping along the middle finger to where the hand meets the wrist, and then continue the tapping process up the pointing finger, following the same route back along the hand, and then along the ring finger, and then along the little finger. Pause for a few seconds before continuing the tapping process down the thumb, beginning at the nail, stopping where the thumb meets the joint of the wrist. It is a good idea to slightly increase the tapping as you move down the thumb. The tapping process encourages the movement of energy along the hand nadis. It is a good idea to concentrate the tapping process a little longer on any area where there is a little tenderness, as this is an indication of some blockage or crystallization of energy.

NADI TECHNIQUE 33: *Ascertaining and Releasing Stress*

Although stress and tension cause prana to congest at various sites in the body, such as in the feet, thighs, shoulders, and neck, it is frequently more apparent in the hands and fingers. To ascertain the level of prana congestion in your hands, start by taking a look at them.

Place both hands, palms down, on the top of the table. Should the veins not protrude slightly at the back of the hands, even when warm, the flow of prana is restricted as a consequence of stress.

Should all the fingers on both hands be fairly close together, this is also a good indication that you are stressed or anxious.

If the overall appearance of the hand is paler than usual, this too suggests the flow of prana has been inhibited as a result of anxiety or stress.

A medical practitioner would most probably give any number of reasons why these things should occur on the hands, but only practice and experience will help you to see exactly what you should be looking for. To help you with your initial analysis, it is probably better to make a study of other people's hands. But the following analysis needs to be carried out on your own hand.

Turn your hand over—the right hand if you are male and the left hand if you are female—with the palm facing upward.

Locate the fleshy part below the thumb, more or less on the joint where the thumb connects to the wrist, and apply some pressure to that spot. This is the junction where the minor nadis connect. Should you feel a little pain or slight discomfort, then this is an indication as to the level of stress. The degree of discomfort will help you ascertain how much pranic congestion has occurred.

Feeling all over that particular area of the fleshy part of the hand, try to locate the exact position. The more specific you are in pinpointing the congested nadi, the more successful you will be when attempting to relieve it.

Now, to treat the problem, turn the appropriate hand over once again, palm flat against the top of the table. With the other hand's index and middle fingers together, locate the bone at the joint of the thumb, more or less on the side of the hand. Applying a little pressure, massage that spot in a clockwise motion, slowly spreading all the fingers on the hand being treated as you do so.

Next, still with a clockwise motion, maintain the massaging process, slowly moving it to the center of the wrist. Continue massaging at this spot for a few moments—as before, applying a little pressure—before slowly moving down the middle of the back of the hand, along the middle finger, stopping when the tip of the nail is reached.

Conclude the process by applying as much pressure as is comfortable to the tip of the nail at the same time as spreading the fingers apart as far as you can until tension is felt in the hand and all the fingers. Maintain this for no longer than thirty seconds, and then relax the hand and suspend the pressure to the middle finger.

Conclude the congestion-releasing process by tapping the middle finger with the middle finger of the other hand, following the same route back to the joint of the thumb at the side of the wrist.

Once you have reached this point, repeat the same process by tapping your way back to the nail tip of the middle finger, and then back again to the starting point at the joint of the thumb at the side of the wrist, and then relax.

Having completed the tapping procedure, repeat the tense and relax exercise, maintaining the tension for a little longer than you previously did. Once this has been carried out, you should relax for a little while, allowing the vitality to circulate.

NADI TECHNIQUE 34: *Relaxation and Breathing*

Relaxation and rhythmic breathing are essential parts of the nadi technique and should be practiced at least once a day.

By now you should have some understanding of the process of relaxation and the way in which rhythmic breathing should be performed. However, this time the whole procedure should be carried out while reclining in a comfortable armchair as opposed to a straight-backed chair.

Before beginning, ascertain your heartbeat by placing your fingers on your pulse and counting with each pulse unit up to six—1, 2, 3, 4, 5, 6; 1, 2, 3, 4, 5, 6; and so on. The units of inhalation and exhalation should always be the same—six pulse units—while the retention and between breaths should always be one-half the number of inhalation and exhalation, or three pulse units. So inhale very slowly a complete breath, counting six pulse units; hold the breath for the count of three; fully exhale to the count of six pulse units, and then count three between breaths, and so on.

Continue this measured breathing for no longer than five minutes, and then relax as completely as you possibly can. Mentally scan your body, relaxing every part of it and making absolutely certain there is no tension at all in the muscles, nerves, tissues, and cells. Spend as much time as is necessary in this relaxation period, resisting any temptation to allow any tension at all to be created.

As always, at the treatment's conclusion, ensure that the body is fully hydrated by drinking a glass of water. However, before

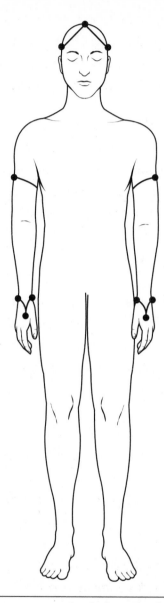

FIGURE 4: *Relieving a stress headache with relaxation nadis on the top of the head, the temples, the upper arms, the wrists, and the backs of the hands.*

consuming the water, pour it from one glass to another, backward and forward, for around a minute or until the water almost comes alive with prana. Putting the water through this pouring process encourages the prana to be activated, ensuring the potency of its vitality.

NADI TECHNIQUE 35: *Instant Relief for Tension*

A problem with tension is that if it's allowed to persist day in and day out, it is likely to ultimately develop into a stressful, anxious state. Sitting at the computer for hours at a time is one of the primary causes of tension headaches and even a stiff neck and back problems.

Whenever we get a tension headache, it's a normal reaction to try relieving it by either rotating our head to loosen the neck muscles or squeezing our forehead and massaging our temples. This only eases a tension headache temporarily, however, and then the majority of people either resort to an analgesic or even a glass of something alcoholic.

One of the most effective nadi techniques for easing a tension headache when all the others fail is this: apply the first (index), middle, and ring fingers of your hand—the left hand if you are a woman, the right if you are a man—to the center of your forehead, just between your brows, and place the middle, third, and little fingers of your other hand at the base of your neck. Apply a little pressure to the forehead and base of your neck simultaneously while massaging the forehead and neck areas in a clockwise motion, gradually increasing the pressure as you massage these points. Maintain the rotational massaging for no longer than a minute, then rest for a few moments before repeating the process. The treatment should be repeated no more than three times for positive results to be achieved.

NADI TECHNIQUE 36: *Relieving a Stress Headache*

Whenever we experience a stressful headache, the first thing we do is apply a little pressure to our forehead to relieve the tension. In fact, we know only too well how nice it is to have someone else do this for us. It's relaxing and nearly always eases the tension. By gently applying pressure to other significant nadi sites, we can also achieve ease, particularly when in the grip of panic.

As shown on the diagram, there are several points that we can apply a little pressure to: the top of the head, the temples, the upper arms, the wrists, and the backs of the hands.

Use your thumb to apply some pressure to the palm of your hand, and use your middle finger, ring finger, and little finger to apply pressure on the back of your hand. Sustain this for about twenty seconds (although the length of time is not that important), and then grip your wrist in your hand and squeeze it as tightly as you can bear, maintaining this for a few seconds, and then release the grip.

Massage the area between your thumb and along that line to your wrist. Apply the same pressure to the area on the upper arms as shown in the diagram.

Get a partner to apply a little pressure to the temples, without rotating. The same can be applied to the crown of the head, although not much pressure is required on this nadi.

Rotating your head with a circular motion and then moving it from side to side is extremely effective, particularly when the head is gently rotated by a partner.

Finally, squeeze your hand as tightly as you can bear, maintaining this for twenty seconds or more if necessary. Apply it to both hands.

Conclude this treatment with some slow, rhythmic breathing, and then relax, not forgetting to drink a glass of freshly charged water at the conclusion of the treatment.

NADI TECHNIQUE 37: *Calming a Panic Attack*

If you are right-handed, apply the tip of your right thumb to the middle finger of your left hand, approximately at the point where the nail connects to the finger, and very slowly increase the pressure until it feels a little uncomfortable. Maintain the pressure for thirty seconds, and then slowly release it. Repeat this at least three times. If you are left-handed, do the same with the middle finger of the right hand.

This is extremely effective in calming the mind when you are in the grip of panic or an anxiety attack. Although power points do not really require any programming in order for them to work, doing so encourages the release of your own personal energies, thus allowing maximum results to be achieved. To program the pressure point, you need to devote at least five minutes of your time each day, sitting quietly while applying the power point to the middle finger and mentally impressing it with your desire to be calmed.

NADI TECHNIQUE 38: *Treating Acute Anxiety Pain*

Anyone who has suffered from stress and anxiety will know only too well how this debilitating condition can cause nonspecific aches and pains in the body. In fact, pain produced by stress can occur anywhere in the body and is not confined to the common tension headache. Panic attacks are often accompanied by morbid thoughts and overwhelming feelings of doom and gloom, throwing the mind into what psychologists term the "adrenaline fear cycle." Once the mind is in this zone, anxiety is perpetuated,

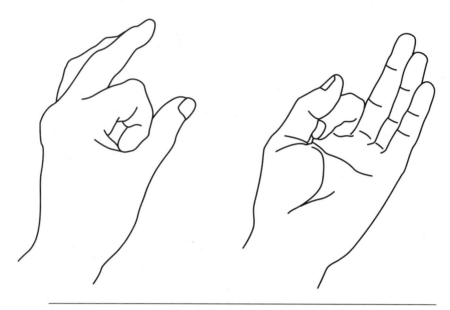

FIGURE 5: *Proper thumb/finger position; the index finger needs to be pressed securely into the thumb joint*

causing all the muscles to tense. It is this constant tension that causes pain to occur.

The power point treatment for this is simple but effective. Sit quietly with your eyes closed, and breathe rhythmically until the rhythm is fully established in your mind. As always, make sure that the inhalations and exhalations are evenly spaced, and focus all your attention on the inflowing and outflowing breath.

When you feel quite relaxed, place the edges of both hands on your lap (little fingers at the bottom) and carefully fold the index fingers of both hands forward to fit snugly between the thumb and the index finger, pushing the thumb against the index finger until the tip of the thumb touches the knuckle of that finger (see figure 5 on the facing page).

Hold this position for at least five minutes to quell the rush of adrenaline and also ease the discomfort of pain. Where pain is concerned, the left hand will ease the right-hand side of the body, and the right hand will ease the left-hand side of the body. Applying the power point simultaneously to both hands produces a stabilizing effect on the brain's pain receptors and has an anesthetizing effect upon the body by affecting the nadis in the hands.

Once this particular power point has been mastered, it can be performed anywhere when in the grip of either panic or the discomfort of pain anywhere in the body.

By now you should have realized that the nadi technique consists of much more than power points and is also an extremely effective psychological program that encourages healing on all levels. While individual health conditions can be treated easily, using selected parts of the nadi technique, you can formulate your own daily regime to maintain the health of mind, body, and spirit.

The fundamental principles of the nadi technique are very simple and work primarily on the ancient precept "physician, heal thyself," simply by tapping in, so to speak, to one's inherent forces. The nadi technique is an ideal holistic system that allows you to dip in and experiment with various methods until you find the one that suits you best.

In this modern age of science and technology, more and more people are turning away from allopathic treatments in favor of the more alternative and less harmful approach. The nadi technique does not involve taking oral remedies but addresses the health from a more subtle level, alleviating and very often curing the condition.

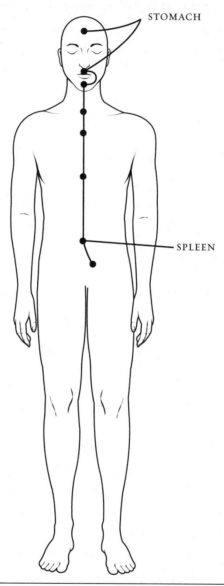

STOMACH

SPLEEN

FIGURE 6: *Stomach nadis*

The power point involving the index finger and thumb is not only effective in easing the pain produced by anxiety, it may also be applied to ease all forms of painful inflammatory conditions, ranging from moderate to acute. Even a toothache can be excruciating at times, and although painkillers can be used as an emergency measure, particularly when a trip to the dentist is not possible, the effects of analgesics quickly wear off. Although some of the nadi technique treatments can be curative where some conditions are concerned, only a trip to the dentist will address the problem of a decaying tooth, so the chosen treatment in this case will only suffice as a temporary measure. And where other persistent painful conditions are concerned, it is always advisable to seek medical advice before using the nadi technique to alleviate pain, just in case the pain is an indication of something more sinister.

NADI TECHNIQUE 39:
Relieving Stomach Pain and Cramps of IBS

As the nadis form an intricate network permeating the entire subtle anatomy, it should come as no surprise that the most unlikely points in the body correspond with the affected parts of the anatomy. There are innumerable nadis feeding the sun center (solar plexus) and digestive and abdominal areas (see figure 6), and discomfort, pain, or cramps can be quickly relieved. These are very often the symptoms produced by irritable bowel syndrome (IBS), today an extremely common condition usually associated with stress.

Locate the point directly in the middle of the palm along the crease of the hand, and apply pressure, sustaining this for as long as is necessary. This will relieve the discomfort of stomach cramps and the pain usually associated with IBS.

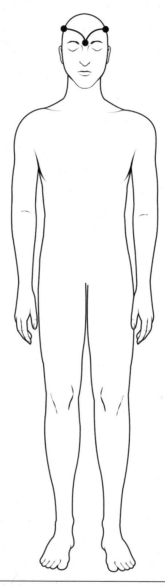

FIGURE 7: *Relieving a migraine*

When discomfort is experienced in the lower abdomen, locate the point on the palm of your hand at the base of the thumb, more or less below the V formed by the middle and index finger, and again apply some pressure and a little massaging.

Headaches and Migraines

It must be said when choosing any alternative medicine technique to treat a health condition, common sense must always prevail and medical advice must always be sought first to rule out the possibility of serious disease. In the case of migraines, acute sufferers must always consult their physician before using any of the techniques given in this book.

Unless you have actually experienced the blinding pain of migraine, then you cannot even imagine how excruciating it can be, forcing the sufferer to retreat to a darkened bedroom. While there are oral treatments available, these rarely bring instant relief. The following treatment is extremely effective.

NADI TECHNIQUE 40: *Relieving a Migraine*

This nadi method is also extremely effective in the treatment of headaches produced by eyestrain or tension caused by sitting at the computer.

Using the tip of the thumb of one hand, position it between the brows, more or less on the bridge of the nose, and gently rub the area upward for a minute before slowly moving to the temples (see figure 7), and then relax for a few moments before repeating the treatment. This is sometimes referred to as Yin Tang in Oriental complementary treatments.

There is always a natural inclination to rub or hold your head, massage your neck, or stretch your shoulders when you have a tension headache. Gently rubbing the area between the brows

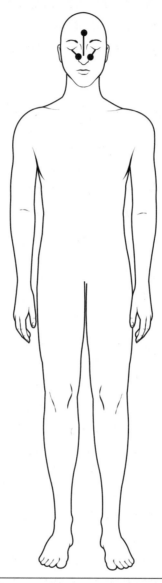

FIGURE 8: *Relieving sinus pain*

in the way given above is really all that is required to ease the pain. Pain is often an indication that the movement of prana is restricted in the nadis, and relief may easily be achieved by gently rubbing the area.

Respiration and Lungs

As a child I used to suffer terribly with sinusitis, the pain of which to a nine-year-old child, let alone an adult, was absolutely unbearable. Although back then I obviously did not know anything at all about the nadi technique, there are some nadi methods that ease the painful condition, such as the following.

NADI TECHNIQUE 41: *Relieving Sinus Pain*

Extend the index finger and middle finger of both hands, and then position them on the bone below both eyes, fairly close to the nose, and gently massage it using a clockwise circular motion.

Maintain the gentle massaging for four to five seconds, then pause briefly before continuing the massaging process. Continue the treatment for five minutes, pausing for a moment between each treatment. This method is usually extremely effective in easing the pain produced by sinusitis. Congestion is also relieved by affecting the nadis in this way.

There is actually no need to follow the nadi technique from beginning to end. Each method is a complete treatment in itself, so you can therefore randomly dip into it and select which treatment suits you best. Of course, some of the methods have been created for specific health conditions, and so this needs to be considered when you are formatting your own holistic program to treat yourself. As someone who has suffered with an incurable respiratory disease since I was three years old, I needed something to increase my overall vitality as well as to improve my breathing capacity. Bronchiectasis requires daily physiotherapy (postural drainage) to clear and prevent the buildup of thick mucus in the lungs, the primary cause of infection. This means the sufferer is constantly exhausted and, in my case, prone to bouts of tiredness accompanied by nonspecific aches in the limbs and glands of the body. Needless to say, since developing and using the nadi technique, I now require little physiotherapy, and although I still suffer from an occasional bout of acute fatigue, these are thankfully few and far between today.

Anyone who suffers with chronic lung disease will know only too well how difficult life can be, especially when there is a flare-up of symptoms and breathing is very difficult. Apart from this, breath is life; life is solely dependent on breath. As I have explained previously, it is during the process of respiration that prana collects in certain bodily centers from where it is continually dispensed throughout the body. The following nadi techniques will not only help to ease the discomfort of a respiratory complaint, but they will also help to ease chest tension and increase the overall vitality in a person suffering with lung disease.

NADI TECHNIQUE 42:
Easing Chest Tension and Helping Breathing

Sit on a straight-backed chair, ensuring that the chest, neck, and head are in as straight a line as possible, with the shoulders thrown slightly back.

Spend a few moments concentrating on your breathing, allowing your stomach to rise as you breathe in and to fall as you breathe out. Remember not to force it or make it a labor, as this will only defeat the whole object of the exercise, which is to improve your breathing and restore your vitality.

Extend your arms horizontally straight out to either side of you, holding that position for no longer than three seconds. Now, fold your right arm in (bending at the elbow) and place your open palm flat against your chest, ensuring that the elbow remains in a horizontal position.

Hold this position for a further three seconds before folding your left arm in (bending at the elbow) and placing the palm of this hand flat against your chest. Hold this position for three seconds.

Once again, extend your right arm horizontally at your side, maintaining this position for no longer than three seconds before folding your arm in once again, with your open palm flat against your chest.

It is a good idea to continue the exercise a little longer if you feel you can do so, otherwise conclude the exercise by breathing deeply in and out a few times, then holding your breath while slapping the palms of both hands against your chest. Relax and rest your hands on your lap.

NADI TECHNIQUE 43:
Simple Way of Relieving Lung Congestion
The dissipation of energy encourages more air to pass into the congested lungs, helping breathing to be easier.

Sitting comfortably on a straight-backed chair, reach over the back of your head with your right hand and simply place your index and middle fingers on the point behind your left ear. Feel the tension in the muscles of your shoulder and shoulder blade, and maintain that position for no longer than three seconds before relaxing.

Now, repeat the process with your left hand, reaching over the back of your head to place your index and middle fingers at the point behind your right ear. Once again, feel the tension in the shoulder muscles and shoulder blade, and maintain that position for no longer than three seconds.

You will have noticed that one of your arms brought more ease to your breathing than the other. Whichever arm it was, repeat the process with the other arm, now holding it in position for six seconds before relaxing with your hands resting on your lap.

NADI TECHNIQUE 44: *Rolling Method*

The rolling method is a most unusual way of releasing congestion in the lungs of anyone who suffers with chronic respiratory conditions and requires daily physiotherapy. Not only does this method ease tension in the chest area, but it also encourages the movement of prana in all the major nadis of the lungs.

Lie flat on the bed without anything to support your head.

Begin some slow, rhythmic breathing, allowing the stomach to rise as you breathe in and to fall as you breathe out.

Next, pull your knees up as close to your chest as you can and clasp your hands around them. Rock yourself backward and forward, increasing the momentum as you do so. Continue the rocking process for at least a minute, taking care not to exhaust yourself, and then relax.

Catch your breath before commencing the rocking process for a further minute, backward and forward, and then from side to side. Relax for a few moments before repeating it again.

Although a little bit different, the rocking motion helps any congestion to be dissipated, allowing sputum to be easily expelled. The rocking process is ideal for a sufferer who does not have anyone to help with physiotherapy. At the conclusion of the rolling method, you should find that the muscles in the chest begin to relax, allowing the breathing to be easier.

NADI TECHNIQUE 45: *Lung Stimulation*

This exercise is an extremely simple yet effective way of stimulating atrophied parts of the lungs, and it is particularly beneficial to smokers or those who have smoked.

For this method you will need to stand up straight, with your legs slightly astride. With your arms by your sides, take a few deep breaths, ensuring that the inhalations and exhalations are evenly spaced, until you feel quite relaxed.

Expel all the air from your lungs as much as possible, and then with the palms of both hands placed gently on your chest, slowly breathe in while gently tapping your chest with all your fingers, as though playing the piano. When the breath is complete, hold it and slap the palms of both hands forcibly against your chest. As you quickly expel all the air from your lungs, allow your body to relax and your shoulders to slouch.

Wait a few moments before repeating. For maximum results to be achieved, the exercise should ideally be performed upon rising in the morning and in the evening before retiring.

As with all exercises of this nature, common sense should always prevail. If you are feeling unwell, then don't perform this technique until you have fully recovered.

As the above exercises stimulate the lungs and encourage the assimilation of vitality in the body, everyone can benefit from them, not just those who suffer with respiratory conditions.

Liver

The liver nadi (not to be confused with the liver meridian) runs from the top of the head, through the right eye, down the middle of the chest, to the right side of the breastbone. It is also located around both ankles and on the edges of the insides of both feet.

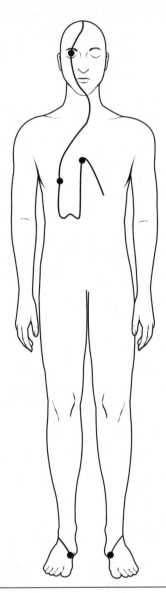

FIGURE 9: *Liver nadis*

This is an extremely sensitive nadi that requires very little manipulation to stimulate.

The liver is an extremely important organ for the maintenance of the health. It is located in the upper right-hand part of the abdominal cavity, beneath the diaphragm and on top of the stomach, right kidney, and intestines. It has multiple functions: it regulates most chemical levels in the blood and excretes a product called bile, which helps to break down fats, preparing them for further digestion and absorption. In fact, all of the blood leaving the stomach and intestines passes through the liver for purification. The liver processes this blood and breaks down the nutrients and drugs in it into forms that are easier to use for the rest of the body. In fact, the liver is believed to perform more than 500 functions; although it is the body's most resilient organ, it needs to be treated with some respect and not be abused.

The nadi treatment helps to detox the liver and help in its overall maintenance. Using figure 9 as a rough guide, with the left hand, gently massage the nadi just below the right side of the ribcage in a clockwise manner; using the right hand, gently massage over the right eye, again with a clockwise motion. Although not absolutely essential, it would help immensely if you carried out the two simultaneously. Maintain this for approximately five minutes.

When this is complete, apply some pressure to the sites on the feet shown in the figure. Apply pressure for thirty seconds, release for three seconds, and then repeat for a further thirty seconds. The treatment should be concluded with drinking a glass of water that has been charged by pouring it through the air from one vessel to another until the water appears to come alive. It is important to pour through the air, thus allowing the water to absorb the prana from the air.

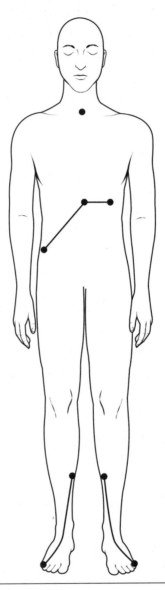

FIGURE 10: *Kidney nadis*

This technique can be used either as a general daily tonic, particularly when you feel sluggish, or when you have overindulged the night before. Results are usually immediate.

Kidneys

The kidneys perform the vitally essential function of removing waste products from the blood and regulating the water fluid levels. The kidneys receive blood through the renal artery, which is then passed through the structure of the kidneys called nephrons, where waste products and excess water pass out of the bloodstream. Their health and efficiency is helped greatly with the nadi technique treatments.

The manipulation of the kidney nadi is effective when there has been infection in the kidneys. There are a few points of treatment with this nadi, and some are more effective than others. Should you be experiencing some tenderness around the back area, it is a good idea to avoid that area initially, at least until you are less sensitive there. In this case, focus your attention on the nadi points on the lower extremities, as shown in figure 10.

First of all, with a downward stroke, using the palms of your hands and applying slight pressure, massage from the point on the lower calf of your leg down your ankle and foot to your little toe. Repeat this several times, allowing your instinct to guide you. It's as simple as that. It's better still if a partner can do it for you while you relax in a comfortable chair.

If you are experiencing no discomfort in your back, gently massage the back area just above your waist, moving the massaging hand round the front to the area just below your ribs. Apply the treatment to both sides. Once again, for obvious reasons, it is more beneficial if a partner applies the treatment.

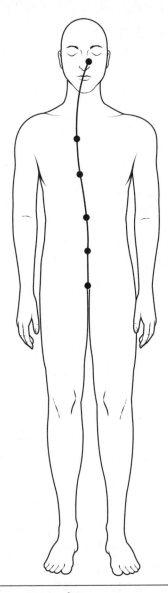

FIGURE 11: *Conception nadis*

It is important to hydrate the body, again by consuming a glass of fresh water charged as described previously.

To help in the maintenance of the kidneys, once you have fully recovered, apply this treatment once a week.

Conception

I fully understand just how sensitive the subject of conception is for many people, particularly if they are having difficulty conceiving.

When one is desperate to have a child, the stress of it usually adds even more complications. Relaxation is extremely important. A quiet, relaxed mind is paramount and encourages a more evenly distributed flow of prana along the appropriate nadis.

Spend at least half an hour relaxing on the bed, focusing on the genital area. Make sure that the inhalations and exhalations of breath are even and that you breathe from the abdominal area as opposed the chest. In fact, this is an extremely important part of the process. Feel the inflowing breath pooling in the lower area of your abdomen. Once the rhythm of your breath has been fully established, after breathing in, hold your breath for the count of six while feeling the power of the inhalation in the genital region. Do this with each inhalation. Try not to strain your breathing or make it a labor, as this merely defeats the whole object of the exercise by adding more tension to the breathing process.

After the half-hour relaxation, using figure 11 as a rough guide, apply a little pressure to your left nostril with the index and middle fingers of your left hand before following a straight line down the front of your body, occasionally prodding strategic points along the nadi until the genital area is reached. Using your index and ring fingers, apply some pressure to the pelvic bone for approximately ten seconds, and then relax.

Repeat the whole process three times, more if you feel a need.

It helps greatly if your partner applies the treatment before and after intercourse.

The object of the exercise is to encourage more prana before, during, and after intercourse. Relaxing with your partner and running through the visualization before intercourse also helps with the precipitation of prana and its arousal.

Meditation and Power Breathing to Treat Respiration

There are innumerable methods of meditation, some of which are quite involved, but the object of nadi meditation is to streamline the subtle channels and create a greater and more meaningful resonance between them and the mind. Meditation is greatly misunderstood by the majority of those who are not familiar with it. It really does not require the practitioner to sit cross-legged and chant *Om* over and over again, although I must say that this is one option.

Seriously, though, speaking as someone who has used various forms of meditation to pull myself successfully from the darkest mire of depression, meditation is most certainly an extremely powerful mental tool. The monastic communities of Tibet and India often consider meditation as the highest form of prayer and the safest way of heightening the awareness by accessing higher states of consciousness. In reality, meditation is a system of mental disciplines used primarily to train the attention to focus on one particular thing to the exclusion of everything else. You may well think this is so easy—until, that is, you try it.

The nadi power meditation consists of a specific mental formula created primarily to encourage the mind to exert greater control over the nadis and the energy flow that passes through them. The resultant formula produces alertness, sharp memory, strong immunity toward illness, and a more energetic approach to life in general. "Why doesn't everyone practice it?" I can hear you say, and my answer to that is this: they most certainly would if they really knew about it.

Let us take a look at the fundamental principles of the nadi power meditation and what the practitioner is expected to do.

The first step is the process of power breathing. We have discussed prana, the universal energy, at some length throughout the book, and power breathing is an integral part of what is known as pranayama, a system of yogic breathing meaning "the control of prana." Power breathing takes a great deal of concentration and effort, and it will only be achieved through determination and practice.

A cautionary note: if you have existing heart or respiratory problems, you must consult your physician before attempting to practice nadi power breathing. In any case, the breathing must not be strained or labored.

It is said that circumstances shape our features and influence the way we think. Particularly in our formative years, our circumstances help to program us in preparation for adult life, and it is only a minority who are sufficiently motivated to mentally break free—if need be—with the overwhelming endeavor to achieve success. This method of power breathing is an ideal tool with which to empower you in your endeavors toward success, happiness, and good health. It involves controlling the breath in a specific way to encourage the rigorous mental regime of clearing all your hangups and negative thoughts. This helps reprogram the subconscious mind.

We live in an extremely fast and very competitive world of science and technology. If you are one of those unfortunate individuals who have not had the benefit of a good and well-balanced upbringing, then at times you may find it an extremely difficult world to live in, and more than likely you choose to live your life as quietly and in the simplest possible way you can. And who can blame you? However, it really does not have to be like that, and it is quite possible to make radical changes to your life and the way you think about everything.

The breathing habits of the Western world really do leave a lot to be desired, and the way we breathe is responsible for many so-called modern-day illnesses, from stress-related conditions to respiratory problems. Breathing correctly can, in fact, help to alleviate anxiety and stress, and by controlling the inhalations and exhalations of our breathing, it is also possible to suspend bodily functions and slow down our thought processes. Get your breathing right, and everything else will be right!

Some systems of yoga regard the whole process of breathing as a precise science and one that is essential for the maintenance of the body's health and equilibrium. Rhythmic breathing also clears the mind and encourages clarity of thought.

NADI TECHNIQUE 46: *Power Breathing*

Sit on a straight-backed chair, making certain that your chest, neck, and head are in as straight a line as possible, with the shoulders thrown slightly back and your hands resting lightly on your lap.

Close your eyes and focus your attention at the tip of your nose. Breathe rhythmically until the rhythm is fully established; when you breathe in, allow your stomach to rise, and when you breathe out, allow it to fall.

Concentrate on your breathing for a few moments longer, making certain that the inhalations and exhalations are evenly spaced but not labored, as this would defeat the whole object of the exercise.

Breathe gently in and out through the nostrils, once again making certain that the process of breathing is not in any way forced.

Inhale steadily with the intention of filling the lower part of the lungs. This is achieved by using the diaphragm to exert a gentle pressure on the abdominal organs by pushing out the front wall of the abdomen.

Next, gently fill the middle part of the lungs by pushing out the lower areas of the ribs, breastbone, and chest.

Follow this process by filling the higher portion of the lungs by gently pushing out the upper part of the chest, including the upper part of the ribcage.

In the final part of the respiratory process, the lower part of the abdomen should be slightly drawn in, thus encouraging more air into the highest part of the lungs.

You should make certain that the inhalations and exhalations are processed smoothly, with no jerkiness between one and the other. Only practice will enable you to master the breathing exercise perfectly, ensuring that the whole process runs smoothly. Only then will maximum benefits be obtained.

You should ideally read through the exercise a few times before attempting it. At first the exercise might appear to consist of three distinct movements, but this assumption is not correct. As explained above, the movement of the breaths should be continuous, with no break at all between them, making it appear as one continuous flow of breath.

Now continue breathing in the way directed above, retaining the breath for a few seconds, again making certain it is not strained.

Exhale slowly, holding the chest firmly in position, at the same time drawing the abdomen in a little and lifting it slowly upward as the breath leaves the lungs.

When the breath has been fully exhaled, relax the chest and abdomen. This process will become easier in time with some practice, and you should then be able to perform it automatically.

Breathing in the above way will encourage the whole respiratory system to work efficiently and will maximize the benefits derived from the air that you draw into your body. The so-called complete breath expands the chest cavity in all directions and is a combination of low, middle, and high breaths, which succeed each other rapidly in the order explained, giving the impression that it is one continuous complete breath.

This is one exercise taken from the system of pranayama breathing methods; again, it should not be strained or made a labor, as this would defeat the whole object of the exercise. As with any such exercise, practice does make perfect. In fact, practice will encourage the exercise to be more efficient and help you to eventually initiate it without any great effort at all. Only then will you be able to achieve the maximum results.

Of course, this particular exercise is only one of many pranayama methods and is an essential part of the nadi technique. Breathing in this way ensures even distribution of prana throughout the subtle energy system, encouraging more vitality and good health. Once you have fully mastered the art of nadi power breathing, the resultant effect on your body will be holistic, and once the levels of prana have been maintained for long periods, the way in which you process thoughts and ideas will greatly improve, and your levels of vitality will also be increased. As well as affecting the body's equilibrium on all levels of consciousness, your senses will also be sharpened, and your perception of the world around you will be heightened as a direct consequence.

Heart and Lungs

Whether you suffer with heart problems or not, the heart and circulation can only benefit from a frequent overhaul of the appropriate nadis. Just as the body benefits from regular exercise, so too do the nadis derive a great deal of benefit from frequent stimulation. Although the nadi technique involves the pressure and stimulation of power points located at strategic sites in the body, the system is not the same as many of the other pressure point therapies such as shiatsu and reflexology, although the underlying principles are fundamentally the same. The nadi technique involves various zone methods and takes into consideration the overall ambiance of the individual's personal energy field.

As the heart is the most important organ in human and animal biology, it needs to be treated with the utmost respect. If it is not working efficiently, then the other organs in the body will understandably suffer as a direct consequence. The heart is an amazing and powerful organ that is capable of withstanding an awful lot. If we treat it well, it will serve us well by maintaining the health and balance of our bodies.

NADI TECHNIQUE 47:
Relieving Chest Discomfort and Pain

The first method stimulates and regulates blood in the chest area and also relieves feelings of pressure, discomfort, and pain in the chest (not heart-related pain).

First of all, locate the appropriate power point by measuring two thumb-widths above the wrist crease in the center of the arm, more or less on the sinewy bone.

You will know immediately that you have located the correct point once you apply a little pressure; you should feel a tingling or other unusual sensation in the chest area.

Using your thumb, apply a little pressure to that point, slowly increasing it for one minute before gradually releasing it. Repeat the process one more time but maintain the pressure now for a little longer than a minute, then gradually release it.

As with all the power points included in the nadi technique, once you have become accustomed to working in this way, you should be intuitively guided to the correct location. It just takes some determination and a lot of practice.

NADI TECHNIQUE 48:
Nourishing and Replenishing the Heart

Not only does this process provide a great deal of nourishment to all aspects of the heart, but it also encourages strong currents of prana to flow freely through the blood, revitalizing and maintaining the heart's overall health.

First of all, with the palm of one hand facing down, locate the bony knob on the outer corner of the wrist. Next, move the finger slightly along from the bony knob and directly to the side of the wrist to locate the small indentation.

Now, with the middle finger, apply pressure on the indentation for thirty seconds, increasing it gradually before slowly releasing the pressure. Repeat this process one more time before resting, and then apply the same process to the other hand.

Now grip the wrist between the middle finger and thumb of the other hand (it doesn't matter if they touch or not), approximately on the crease that separates the hand from the wrist, maintaining this for a further thirty seconds before relaxing.

Conclude the process by tapping all over the back of the hand at random points, beginning with the bony knob at the edge of the wrist.

You should feel quite invigorated with this nadi procedure and may even experience a slight tingling sensation or warm feeling across the chest and down the arms. Occasionally you may feel overwhelmed with a feeling of complete calm.

Performed on a regular basis, the nadi heart-nourishing and replenishing treatment will encourage a more efficient heart as well as improve the efficiency of the circulation.

Although the nadi technique approaches the process of healing holistically, it still consists of principles that can be used to address problems with specific organs. Today cardiothoracic problems are quite prevalent, with diseases such as emphysema, asthma, angina, chronic bronchitis, and any number of chronic heart conditions, which account for millions of deaths worldwide every year. The treatment for respiratory conditions is quite diverse, ranging from steroid inhalers and tablets to oxygen and other nebulized treatments. As with the majority of treatments, side effects frequently occur, but the nadi technique produces no side effects whatsoever and can often bring instantaneous relief. In some cases, a nadi technique treatment can ease the symptoms permanently, if not cure the condition completely.

When some pain or discomfort is experienced when pressure is applied to a power point, it is considered to have excessive energy; when the pressure produces a degree of comfort, the nadi is deficient in energy. Although diagnostically the nadi technique is similar to other pressure-point therapies, the nadi technique addresses the problems of illness and disease at many different

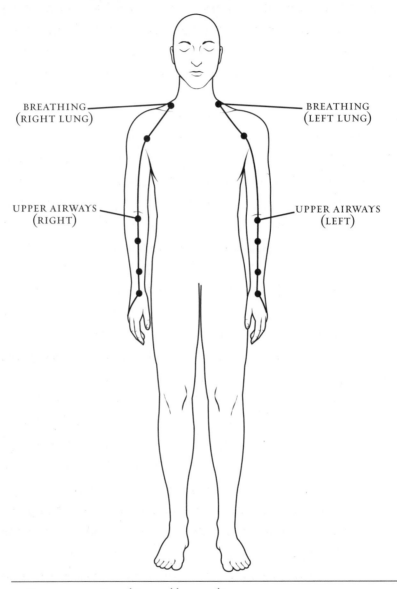

FIGURE 12: *Breathing and lung nadis*

levels. When a person is experiencing some difficulty breathing, perhaps as a consequence of congestion resulting from a chest infection, there are various ways of relieving the discomfort, all of which I have used on myself over the years with some degree of success.

NADI TECHNIQUE 49: *Relief from Lung Congestion*

Writing as someone who has suffered with an incurable lung disease (bronchiectasis) since I was three years old, I know only too well the importance of correct breathing and instant relief when the breathing is restricted for some reason. The nadis that convey prana directly from the upper airways extend from the side of the neck, down the arms, and to the hands. There is absolutely nothing worse than lung congestion, and there is an extremely simple yet effective way of bringing relief to the breathing when you are experiencing some difficulty.

First, raise your right arm and place the open hand across the left ear, holding it there for a count of five while taking a deep breath, and then relax. Now do the same with the left arm, placing the hand over the right ear, again for the count of five, taking a deep breath, and then relaxing. (I only suggest the count of five as one option, as raising your arm in this way, particularly when your breathing is labored, can be a little exhausting.)

This simple procedure helps to relax the muscles in the upper-chest area, and the inhalation encourages the movement of prana along the appropriate nadis.

For the following treatment you will need to enlist the help of a partner.

Sit comfortably on a straight-backed chair with your hands on your lap. Take a few deep breaths, again making sure not to strain it or make it a labor.

Using figure 12 as a guideline, your partner should place their middle three fingers on either side of your neck, more or less in the hollow where it meets the shoulders, and then apply a little pressure. Maintain the pressure for a few seconds before moving the hands to the fronts of the shoulders, again applying some pressure.

Maintaining the pressure, your partner's hands should move down the arms to the wrists, at which point they should grip the wrists tightly, again maintaining the grip for a couple of seconds before slowly letting go.

Now either you or your partner should massage the palm of your left hand before squeezing it tightly between the thumb and fingers, and then apply the same treatment to the right hand.

Now take hold of your left thumb, making certain that you grip it from the joint, and maintain the pressure for five seconds. Do the same with the right thumb, and then relax.

To conclude the treatment, simply raise your arms and lock your hands around the back of your neck, lifting your elbows as high as you can and stretching your arms. Maintain that position while taking a few deep breaths, and then relax.

As with the other treatments, drink a glass of mineral water charged in the way previously explained.

With this treatment, slow, rhythmic breathing is imperative, as this precipitates the movement of prana along the nadis, encouraging the blood supply to the lungs.

The Mind

The nadi technique works solely on the premise that we are far more than a biological unit comprised of innumerable groups of cells that collectively have a life expectancy of threescore years and ten. Because lifestyles have radically changed, people are now living lives far in excess of seventy years—today seventy has become the new fifty. Unless one has a genetic predisposition to a life-threatening disease, there is no reason why one cannot enjoy the longevity of a healthy life and live at the very least to one hundred years old. Even so, the nadi technique can very often encourage the healing of a genetically inherited disease and help to suspend or alleviate it, if not affect a complete cure. It is all a matter of attitude.

The human body itself is an incredible source of self-created power that consists of a subtle energy system capable of assimilating and distributing an extraordinary force through a process that affects everything and everyone that comes within its parameters. In the same way that an automobile engine will not function efficiently when one of its components ceases to work, so the human biology is also greatly affected when disease occurs in one of its organs.

We have already examined how the cells and organs of the body may be influenced by the mind, and how our mind can exert great control over our bodily functions to encourage order and harmony throughout the cells. This process really does give a whole new meaning to the term "mind over matter" and explains perfectly well that you are what you think. I am not suggesting that such mind control can be achieved overnight. On the contrary, to enable the healing of any disease to occur, a great deal of training is required beforehand. There would be little use in training the mind when serious disease is already well and truly established in the body. A person should undergo such training when healthy as opposed to when sick; this would be like closing the gate when the horse has already bolted. However, this is not to say that a person with an extremely positive mind would not be capable of affecting some sort of cure when they are suffering with some sort of disease. Such miraculous cures have been documented, albeit on rare occasions.

One man who believed totally in the development of the mind's latent abilities to cure forgetfulness, depression, and many phobias was William Joseph Ennever. In fact, Ennever believed in the process of training the mind so much that in 1890 he created the Pelmanism system, consisting of numerous exercises to encourage the mind to be stronger and more efficient. Ennever was not at all surprised when his so-called new thought techniques attracted a great deal of interest, particularly amongst the world of celebrities. The Pelmanism Institute was established in London and New York and attracted such notable people as British Prime Minister Herbert Asquith, Lord Robert Baden Powell (founder of the Boy Scout Movement), writer Rider Haggard, and playwright Jerome K. Jerome, to mention but a few. Although little is known about the mind, of one thing we can rest assured: its efficiency and overall performance can most certainly be developed.

Take the memory, for example; anyone who is in the habit of writing copious lists of everything they need to remember, forever announcing that they have awful memories, is unwittingly making the memory lazy and inefficient. In fact, the more the memory is used, the stronger and more efficient it becomes. There is no such entity as a poor memory, only a lazy one. In fact, the memory's performance is surprisingly adversely affected by white flour and sugar products and is also greatly impaired by nicotine, which interferes with the flow of prana along the nadis. (As an aside, smoking's impact on the metaphysical as well as the physical health is immense; it creates innumerable health problems in the long term and greatly shortens the smoker's life.)

The way in which the mind processes thoughts and feelings may be improved easily with the use of simple exercises specifically designed to encourage the development and cultivation of the faculties. Increasing the mind's capacity produces a holistic effect upon the health and encourages a much greater control over one's life.

First of all, it is imperative that the mind is calm and the body is relaxed. An anxious person's subtle energies are quickened by the levels of adrenaline they have allowed to be released into their body. Anxiety quickens the neurological processes, and as a consequence produces an adverse effect on the nadis and the subtle energies. Some people find it extremely difficult to relax even in bed at the end of the day. Today it is common knowledge how anxiety affects the health if allowed to persist, and just how ill worrying over something makes us feel. It causes our head to throb and every muscle in our body to ache. In fact, if you persist in this mental state, you begin to think that something untoward is occurring in your body.

The nadi technique of alleviating the symptoms that are nearly always produced by anxiety is extremely effective and requires very little effort on the practitioner's part. Once the body is relaxed and the mind fairly quiet, then you are in the correct zone of receptivity.

Although meditation is an excellent tool for strengthening the overall efficiency of the mind, it really all depends on which technique is actually used. What method of meditation suits one person may not be suitable for another, and so if you want to use meditation as a means of dealing with your levels of stress, then it really must be one you enjoy doing and one you enjoy doing with great ease. However, for now, let us explore some mental exercises for encouraging a stronger and more efficient mind.

NADI TECHNIQUE 50:
The Stroop Effect for Mind Efficiency

First of all, let us take a look at the Stroop experiment. Although I do not use this for the purpose it was originally intended by John Stroop, I have always found it an effective way of encouraging focus and concentration. Used on a regular basis, it improves alertness and overall efficiency of the mind.

The Stroop Effect, as it is known, was created by American psychologist John Ridley Stroop as a color word task to demonstrate the reaction of the time it takes to perform a task.

Words such as *red, blue, green, orange,* and others are written in two ways: using the colors that the words represent and using colors that do not denote the words. The majority of people have no problems whatsoever reading the word in the correct color but encounter some difficulty reading the word when it is in a different color altogether.

First of all, test your mental agility by reading the words in their correct colors as quickly as you can a few times, backwards and forwards. For example, write all the colors down in the colors they denote, such as *red* written in red, *blue* written in blue, and so on, and then try reading the letters written in different colors, such as *red* written in blue, *blue* written in red, and so on. The more you practice this, the more proficient you will become at mastering the psychological task.

Of course, there are innumerable other effective ways of exercising the mind to increase its capacity and improve its performance and agility, as in our next technique.

NADI TECHNIQUE 51:
The Cupboard Method for Memory Recall

An extremely effective method for improving the memory is called the cupboard method. I have always used this, particularly when I am stressed or overworked. The cupboard method is an extremely simple way of encouraging recall and improving the overall efficiency of the memory.

Initially, you must spend at least ten minutes a day mentally creating the image of a cupboard. If you like, you can use a cupboard in your home, or even one you have seen, as an example. Whatever you do, visualize the cupboard with your eyes closed until you can see every minute detail clearly in your mind. Make it brightly colored until it looks almost cartoonlike. Doing this will impress your mind more strongly and make it easier to visualize. No matter what the mental image of your cupboard looks like, once you have created it, do not change it in any way. In fact, know everything about your cupboard so that you can recall it in an instant.

Put the cupboard method to a test. At night before you climb into bed, sit quietly and allow your cupboard to appear in your mind. Turn your cupboard slowly in your mind and look at it from all angles. See it very clearly and know everything about it.

Once you are confident that the cupboard is fully established in your mind, mentally pull back the door and look inside. See the shelves and fix them firmly in your mind.

Next, place on the shelves all the things you need to remember the next day. It doesn't matter how many things you place in your cupboard as long as you are mindful of exactly what you are doing. Place each thing carefully, one at time, in the appropriate place.

Once you have placed everything securely in place, take a good look at each thing (whatever it is) and then very slowly close the door.

Lie or sit for a few moments longer, mentally thinking about the contents of the cupboard. Then dissolve it all from your mind and either go about your chores or go to sleep.

Upon waking in the morning, sit quietly for a few minutes with your eyes closed before allowing your cupboard to be established in your mind. Watch the cupboard for a few moments, and then very slowly pull the door open.

You may not see anything to begin with, but within a few moments the things you have placed in it will pop, one after the other, into your mind. It never fails.

The cupboard method is not only an effective way of improving the efficiency and performance of the memory, but in the long term it also encourages the mind to be more focused. It is an effective process of visualization that involves the image-making faculty of the brain and encourages an increase in the overall awareness.

NADI TECHNIQUE 52:
Power Meditation for Mind Efficiency

This two-part exercise involves two circles, one white and one black. The object of the exercise is to train the image-making faculty of the brain and encourage the way in which it processes data to be much more efficient.

Sit quietly for a few moments, ensuring that the mind is more or less still and the body is quite relaxed.

Spend a few minutes breathing rhythmically, and as you breathe in, say to yourself, "I breathe in," and when you breathe out, say "I breathe out." You may think this quite unnecessary, but it is an essential part of the process of preparing the mind. By sending verbal or silent instructions to yourself—it really doesn't matter which—you produce a positive affirmation to your subconscious mind.

When you feel mentally prepared, imagine a large white circle in front of you. Focus your attention on the circle for a few moments, and then very gradually see a black dot in the center of the white circle. Now, focus your attention on the black dot, at the same time keeping the white circle in the peripheral line of vision.

Maintain this image for no longer than one minute, and then watch the black dot slowly expanding, more and more, until it eventually covers the white circle completely.

Now focus your attention totally on the black circle for no longer than sixty seconds, and then see in its center a white dot. Focus your attention on the white dot for a further sixty seconds, and then watch the white dot slowly expand until it eventually covers the black circle completely.

Repeat the whole process for no longer than fifteen minutes. Even if you find the exercise laborious, it is important to persevere. Once you fully master this technique of visualization, you should find meditation itself so much easier to do.

The white/black circle exercise encourages the overall efficiency of your mind and also helps the performance of your memory. I have also found it quite an effective exercise for encouraging the image-making faculty when one has some difficulty with the process of visualization. Used regularly, it really does produce a remarkable effect on all mental skills.

If you are one of those people who simply finds it impossible to visualize and encounters too many difficulties when endeavoring to visualize the white and black circles, here's another way to do the exercise.

Make the two circles out of card stock in their respective colors, white and black, and then draw a black dot in the center of the white circle, and a white dot in the center of the black circle.

Prop the cards up in front of you, no more than two feet away and as near to eye level as possible. Make certain the lighting is fairly subdued, ensuring that there is sufficient light for the circle to be clearly seen. Candlelight is ideal, and this also creates just the right ambiance for meditation. Further set the mood by playing some appropriate music and perhaps burning some pleasant incense.

As before, spend a few minutes with your eyes closed, breathing rhythmically to relax your body and make the mind quiet. Always make sure that the back, chest, and head are in as straight a line as possible, with the shoulders thrown slightly back and the hands resting lightly on your lap. All this may seem fairly repetitive, but it is a prerequisite for meditation, and it is therefore essential that you fix it all firmly in your mind until rhythmic breathing becomes second nature.

Open your eyes and fix your gaze on the black dot in the center of the white circle. Resist the temptation to blink or move your eyes away even for a moment.

When your eyes begin to tear, close them and allow the afterimage to come into your mind, which will usually be in the complementary color, black or gray.

To retain the afterimage for as long as you can, commence breathing slowly and deeply, making certain that the inhalations and exhalations are evenly spaced and the whole process is not forced or strained in any way, as this will defeat the whole object of the exercise.

When the afterimage becomes fragmented and begins to fade, open your eyes and move your gaze to the white spot in the center of the black circle, and simply repeat the whole process. Continue the exercise for as long as you feel comfortable, alternating from one to the other.

As previously explained, the circle exercise helps to improve the way in which the mind processes data, greatly increasing its overall performance, sometimes as much as 70 percent. The circle meditation is also an extremely powerful mental device that helps to control neurological activity and in the long term encourages the overall health to improve. With increased mental alertness comes heightened awareness and determination, followed by success. This mental process stimulates the neurological receptors and encourages the efficiency of the mind. In the long term, this improves the way data is processed by the brain and promotes sharpness and clarity of thinking.

6

Food and Nutrition
Spiritual Revolution &
Health Consciousness

The nadi technique also considers the food we eat. Food is not only an excellent energy source; a correct and healthy diet encourages the overall efficiency of our body and produces good health. A poor diet makes the body inefficient and, in the long term, causes problems to arise with our health. After all, as the saying goes, we are what we eat, as much as we are what we think.

A now well-known Theosophical precept that "God's law is evolution" explains perfectly well why today it would seem that there is some sort of spiritual revolution occurring all over the planet. I would prefer to call it a spiritual revival, as it is my opinion that humanity is simply beginning to remember what it has long since forgotten. Mankind is now on the point of struggling from beneath the crushing burden of matter that weighs it down and is now moving quickly toward the light, rather like a huge invisible swan whose wings flap noiselessly across the surface of a great ocean.

Today more and more people are taking care of themselves by becoming more mindful of the food they consume. This growing health consciousness is a clear indication that the planet is undergoing some sort of spiritual metamorphosis. Such a transformation in the way the human race is now beginning to evolve will have a far-reaching effect upon the future of the planet as a whole. The planet itself is a living organism, and like the human form it too requires sustenance to sustain it—sustenance produced by the mind and the cultivation of correct thinking and total respect toward its ecology. And once the realization dawns upon the human race that the planet itself lives and breathes, the universe will then begin to respect the human race in return. The way we conduct our lives today will most certainly set an example to those who shall be born tomorrow and who will be the guardians of a Golden Age. And although today there is still a minority of the human race who do not care for the planet and who also have little regard for their fellow man, the collective consciousness of humankind continues to expand like the swelling waters of a dammed river during a storm.

Just like the human organism, the planet too possesses a subtle anatomy, and although its vibratory tones do equate to the human chakra system, its unique organization creates a different resonance at strategic locations across the uneven terrain of the planet. It may well be that our prehistoric forebears possessed some knowledge of this when they erected their Neolithic and Bronze Age monuments and megaliths at strategic places of burial and worship, and perhaps that is the very reason why temples and monasteries were later erected at specific locations— because the earth energies were more prevalently powerful there. Today little or no consideration is given to where exactly important structures are erected and how the overall ambiance of a location can affect an individual psychologically and spiritually. Would that we could know exactly what our prehistoric ancestors knew about the effects of earth energies upon the human mind; then the world in which we presently live would no doubt be a much happier and more harmonious place.

The nadi technique considers the significant connection between the planet and humankind, and accepts that there is no divide between the two. As our bodies thrive on a healthy diet, so too does the planet flourish with our respect and care.

There is today a consensus of opinion that we are what we eat, and the food we consume influences our actions as well as affects the way we think. Having not eaten meat since I was thirteen, I now find the very thought of eating the flesh of an animal repulsive. It is a medical fact that red-meat eaters are more volatile and much more likely to develop some sort of cancer in later life. Apart from this fact, it is widely accepted that the flesh of animals contains the elements of fear that overwhelmed them when their life was cruelly ended in the abattoir. The adrenaline produced by fear persists after death in the flesh of all creatures, and to some extent this adrenaline is apparent in meat, even when it is cooked. Adrenaline is a stimulant, and when it is consumed in meat, it can produce symptoms similar to anxiety, paranoia, and stress.

These are just some of the adverse effects caused by eating meat and other animal products, but apart from these there are many other reasons why a carnivore should consider a meatless diet, and not only because meat is not good for the health. Spiritual implications arise from consuming the flesh of any living creature, and although a meatless diet does not appeal to everybody's digestion, the benefits of not eating meat in the long term really do cover a broad spectrum biologically, psychologically, and spiritually. The nadi technique is much more than a system of holistic healing; once fully understood, it becomes almost a way of life and ultimately affects every aspect of your being. The quality of the food we eat and the thoughts we think are reflected in the colors and intensity of the bioluminescence of our aura. Although such effects are usually transitory, unless we make radical changes to our lives by thinking differently and adopting a healthier way of eating, the impact on our personal energy field will eventually become permanent.

A person who has spent a lifetime eating chemically enhanced food and thinking negative thoughts wrongly assumes that they are far too old to change their ways. This is not true; any change, however small, is a start where the nadi technique is concerned. The nadi technique is about understanding how energy may be controlled in the body to enhance the quality of your life. Once your health begins to improve, it will reflect in everything you do. This book is not a religious system as much as it is a philosophical system, and it was written to transform the way you think, not to convert you to a different faith.

We are constantly peopling our own private portion of space with the thoughts we produce, and our thoughts become either the powerful force that sustains the health of the planet upon which we live or the perpetrator of its gradual deterioration and ultimate demise.

To the majority of people, the very suggestion that the planet is a living organism is a little too metaphysical and conceptually far-fetched and fanciful. Nonetheless, as we move further into the modern age of science and technology, it is a theory that has to be taken seriously. It is now a scientific, environmental fact that industry and humankind's general abuse have greatly contributed to a remarkable deterioration in the earth's atmosphere, and although skeptics have dismissed this as "scaremongering," we only have to take a look at the way nature itself is now behaving.

The nadi technique is about promoting balance in the body, which will, in the long term, be reflected upon the external world of earth, sky, and human habitations. Our health is very often a reflection of how we think, and the way we think in turn ultimately affects our planet. There are rivers of vitality streaming through the veins of the planet in the ongoing process of maintaining harmony and balance and sustaining its life, just as the network of nadis permeates our bodies in the maintenance of health. As a consequence of man's ignorance and cruelty toward each other, at strategic points across the planet these rivers of vitality are beginning to silt over, and just like the decreasing waters of a neglected lake, the energy that sustains our world is slowly failing.

For many years now, my wife, Dolly, has made an extensive study of the effects of food on our health. Her observations were made through her work in corporate hospitality and also cooking for huge events all over the UK. The following information, including the appendix, is from her.

Energy Foods to Maintain Balance

Before I move on to the healing powers of foods that are connected to the chakras, everybody should have the basic knowledge of a balanced diet.

Protein: These form enzymes that control chemical reactions throughout the body. Each molecule is composed of amino acids, which the body needs to produce new protein (protein retention) and to replace damaged proteins (maintenance).

Because there is no protein storage provision in the body, amino acids must always be present in the diet. Excess amino acid is usually discarded in the urine. About twenty amino acids are found in the body, and about ten of these are essential. Amino acids are particularly important during the early development of pregnancy and lactation, when growing up, and especially in healing. Children require more protein than adults, as they are constantly producing new tissue, and the lack of protein can result in stunted growth and impair mental development.

Sources of dietary protein include red meats, tofu, soy products, eggs, legumes, and dairy products. The bases of many cultural diets take two incomplete protein sources to make one complete protein source—for example, rice and beans.

Saturated fats: Coming from animal sources, saturated fats have been a staple food in many world cultures—for example, butter and lard. They are found in dairy foods and also in palm oil, coconut oil, and cocoa butter. A high intake of saturated fats leads to heart disease.

Unsaturated fats: They have a protective effect on the heart. They occur in two forms, polyunsaturated and monounsaturated, and are found in all vegetable oils. Monounsaturated fats are typically liquids such as olive, flaxseed, peanut, and sesame oils. Polyunsaturated fats are soybean, corn, and sunflower oils. They contain linolenic acids, the fatty acids that cannot be made by the body.

Trans fats: These are rare in nature and have been shown to be very detrimental to human health, but they are useful in the food-processing industry for things like rancidity resistance.

Vegetarians, as my husband and I are, eat a diet that is lower in fat than a standard diet, but sometimes this diet can be fattier with the inclusion of cheese being a full-fat dairy product. You can always use lowfat cheese. The same can be said of meat eaters. If you make a meat-based soup, stew, or sauce, make it the day before and store it in the refrigerator overnight so the fat content will rise to the top and solidify. Just scoop it off and throw it away. Little things like this can make a great difference to your life and health.

Dietary fiber: Fiber helps reduce gastrointestinal problems such as constipation and diarrhea by increasing the weight and size of a stool and then softening it. Whole-wheat flour, nuts, and vegetables stimulate peristalsis, the rhythmic muscular contractions of the intestines that move foods along the digestive tract. Foods that are high in fiber are filling and low in fat, and more importantly they take longer to eat and therefore make you feel fuller for longer. Fiber is a range of plant materials that the body cannot digest. They pass through the body undamaged until they reach the large intestine, where they react in different ways.

SOLUBLE FIBER: Soluble fiber dissolves in water in the intestinal tract to produce a gel-like substance that slows the movement of food within the intestines. This helps lower blood glucose levels because it slows the absorption of sugar. Fiber, especially from whole grains, is thought to lessen insulin spikes and therefore reduces the risk of type 2 diabetes. There is a link between increased fiber consumption and decreased risk of colorectal cancer, although this is still being investigated. Sources include peas, beans, root vegetables, citrus fruits, and oat bran.

INSOLUBLE FIBER: Insoluble fiber absorbs water, which adds bulk to fecal matter in the bowel and helps to move waste products more quickly. Insoluble fiber is fermented by bacteria in the bowel to produce fatty acids that nourish the intestinal wall. By speeding it up, it prevents toxins from coming into prolonged contact with the intestinal wall, and this could prevent cancer of the lower bowel. Insufficient insoluble fiber is thought to contribute to constipation, hemorrhoids, and diverticulitis. Sources are wheat, rice, bran, whole grains, cereals, bread, and nuts.

Both types of fiber can be found in peas, apples, bananas, barley, pears, prunes, and cabbages.

Fatty acids: These are a complex matter, but we do know that omega-3 and omega-6 fatty acids are important to health. Both of these omega long-chain polyunsaturated fatty acids are substrates—molecules upon which enzymes act—which have been shown to reduce cholesterol and reduce the ability to clot and clog up the arteries. In some respects they are hormones, with omega-3 coming from marine sources—for instance, ocean fish such as mackerel, herring, tuna, sardines, and salmon—and omega-6 is a building block for series 1 prostaglandins, which have anti-inflammatory properties.

Carbohydrates: Classified as monosaccharide (glucose), disaccharides (glucose and fructose), or polysaccharides (starch), depending on the number of sugar units they contain. Carbohydrates are mainly rice, noodles, and bread and grain products.

Minerals: The chemical elements required by living organisms other than the four elements of carbon, hydrogen, oxygen, and nitrogen, which are present in nearly all organic molecules. They can be supplied by the foods in which they occur naturally, but they are often artificially added to the diet as supplements, such as iodine in iodized salt, which prevents goiter, the swelling of the thyroid gland. (Selenium deficiency is considered also to be a contributing factor.)

Micro minerals: Known as bulk minerals—for instance, calcium for muscle, the digestive system, and bone strength. Magnesium builds bone and increases flexibility, and phosphorous is essential for energy processing.

Copper: An essential trace element that stimulates the immune system to fight infections, repair tissues, and promote healing. Copper also helps to neutralize free radicals, which can cause severe damage to the cells. It is also essential in the normal growth and development of human fetuses, infants, and children. The sources are seafood (especially shellfish), organ meats, whole grains, legumes, beans, lentils, and unsweetened chocolate. Copper is also found in nuts (especially cashews), wheat, rye, lemons, raisins, kale, coconut, papaya, and apples.

Well-known legumes include alfalfa, clover, peas, beans, lentils, carob, soy, peanuts, vanilla, and radishes. Legumes contain relatively low quantities of the essential amino acid methionine, but if an adequate amount of protein is consumed as well, then there isn't a problem—e.g., daal with rice, beans with corn tortillas, tofu with rice, and peanut butter with wheat bread.

Phytochemicals: These trace chemicals are typically found in plants, especially fruits and vegetables, in their thousands, but are also in other organisms including seafood, algae, and fungi. Phytochemicals are compounds that have evolved to help plants resist pests and ultraviolet light. They have been rigorously tested by the World Health Organization.

One of the main classes of phytochemical is polyphone anti-oxidants, known to provide certain health benefits to the cardiovascular system and the immune system. There are various arguments as to credible evidence of various phytochemicals—for instance, the possible benefits of cancer prevention, where phytochemicals can cut off capillaries that deliver nutrients to developing tumors. This is a highly complex matter where one phytochemical can prevent the uptake of another and therefore reduce the health benefits. You can see this daily in the news where some foods or liquids that you knew or thought were bad for you are now reported to be beneficial. An example of this is alcohol; it is now thought that one or two glasses of wine (a flavonoid) are a general antioxidant and are useful in the prevention of arteriosclerotic vascular disease.

Some of the most controversial phytonutrients, high in content, have been marketed as "super foods." These are foods that are considered to be especially nutritious or beneficial to health or well-being. Since 1 July 2007, the marketing of products as super foods is prohibited in the EU unless supported by credible medical evidence. Many of you may remember when super foods first became known, and we all thought that a shot of pure wheat grass was so good for us—until it digested and led to a stomach disorder, and we realized that it was far too strong for us in a pure state.

When we look at food, we must use common sense and know that a poor diet will lead to obesity, cardiovascular disease, diabetes, and osteoporosis. It really doesn't matter how little or how much you have to spend on food in your weekly shopping; you are the architect of your own destiny, and you can buy a portion of fries for the same price as buying some carrots and other ingredients to make a carrot soup. This doesn't mean that we should not buy a portion of fries; it just means that for the rest of the week we should balance them with a nutritious diet. Some people may want to take this further and learn how individual foods have so many different benefits to our health. We know that blueberries, for instance, are high in antioxidants, anthocyanins, vitamin C, manganese, and the dietary fiber compound pterostilbene, which protects the heart in the same way as cholesterol-lowering drugs; goji berries are the same, although you may not find these as plentiful as blueberries in your local supermarket.

Today it may be hard to arrive home from our hectic lives and cook a meal from scratch, but with some time management we can cook a fresh soup to last for a couple of days or make a bean stew and freeze half, and so on. It is also important to buy the most minimally processed foods, especially if you have children. Yes, it would be lovely to fill our children's lunch boxes with some berries, nuts, seeds, fruits, and an oily fish sandwich, but they probably wouldn't speak to us again! We always have to compromise with children, but putting them on the proper food path in their youngest years, however hard it is, will benefit them for a lifetime and give them a fighting chance against disease. It will also be a continuous path from generation to generation.

Many of you may think that if you take vitamins to compensate for a poor diet you are protecting yourself, but in fact some vitamins as a supplement may be harmful. For instance, beta carotene obtained from food is known to prevent cancers, but as a separate food supplement, especially in vitamin A form, it may actually contribute to cancers. It is important to keep up with the news on bona fide medical studies of certain foods and have an open mind; do not listen to the interpreted version of these reports in a tabloid newspaper.

Remember, as with all things in this life, balance is the key.

APPENDIX

Chakra-Energizing Foods

As we know, chakras are subtle centers in the biological system of a living organism that take in and give out energy. Health is determined by the flow of energy for the seven chakras into the metabolic network of our bodies. If the energy is blocked, it will restrict energy flow to the chakras and lead to illness. Foods that are connected to the colors of the chakras carry vibrations that activate or balance your chakras, not only energizing you but also protecting your immune system.

You must remember that we are all unique, with complexities and very different environments, and what works for one person may not work for another. You must listen to your body and mind when balancing your chakras; you are the architect of your own destiny. I have to say that a concentrated soup or a blended fruit juice may energize one person but unfortunately may affect another in an adverse way, such as resulting in some time on the toilet. If pure foods are not your normal diet, then please be sensible; for example, try them during times you do not have a heavy work schedule. Please do not give up if some foods affect you in this way; just gradually introduce them in your diet and let your body get used to them.

Here I am going to include many recipes that are linked to our chakra system. They can be made in advance for one person or used at a dinner party. Each one of my chakra soups will balance each particular chakra, and I will also explain why and what parts of the body for which they are beneficial. I am including main dishes, side dishes, and desserts here too so that you can have a chakra dinner party and educate your friends and family on the vital importance of the chakras and how food plays such an important part in not only the chakras but your physical and mental well-being.

The Chakras and the Food of Life

Red: Root (Muladhara) Chakra

- Strawberries, red kidney beans, tomato, beet, watermelon, red grape, red pepper, red cabbage, pomegranate, horseradish, chilies, rhubarb, red lentils
- Red spices, cayenne pepper, ginger, cinnamon

Many of these red foods contain lycopene, which reduces the onset of prostate cancer, lowers blood pressure, and reduces tumor growth.

Imbalances of the root chakra result in lower back pain, sciatica, circulatory problems in the legs and feet, and depression.

Red wine, in moderation, contains antioxidants; in particular, the skin of the red grape curbs the effects of aging and contains the anticancer and anti-inflammatory compound resveratrol, which is also present in blueberries, cranberries, and peanuts.

Red kidney beans are packed with fiber, potassium, and zinc, which all reduce cholesterol, which protects against heart disease. Dried beans have as much protein weight for weight as a fillet steak, but obviously with more health benefits. Ginger is known as an antiemetic to prevent and control all kinds of nausea.

Orange: Sacral (Svadisthana) Chakra

- Orange, papaya, yam, carrot, cantaloupe, apricot, mango, pumpkin, butternut squash, orange pepper
- Ginger, cumin, turmeric

The underground stems of turmeric contain compounds that have been shown to reduce inflammation and have a protective effect on the liver.

Many orange foods contain beta carotene, flavonoids, lycopene, and vitamin C. These reduce age-related macular degeneration and prostate cancer.

Sacral chakra imbalances can lead to problems with the urinary tract, impotency, frigidity, yeast infections, kidney malfunctions, and lower-abdominal problems.

Yellow: Solar Plexus (Manipura) Chakra

- Lemon, corn, eggs, bananas, yellow pepper, pineapple, cauliflower, polenta, melons, swede (rutabaga), grapefruit, ginger, yellow courgettes (zucchini)
- Saffron, fenugreek

Imbalances of the solar plexus chakra can lead to digestive problems, ulcers, diabetes, constipation, and colitis.

Green: Heart (Anahata) Chakra

- Lime, lettuce, spinach, green pepper, avocado, artichoke, peas, asparagus, cabbage, cucumber, seaweed, broccoli, kale, olives, leeks, fennel, green beans, green courgettes (zucchini), Brussels sprouts, green grapes, sugar snap peas, pears, apples, pak choi (bok choy), kiwi

- Mint, chives, bay leaf, parsley, basil

Many green foods contain chlorophyll, fiber, folate, and vitamin C. They reduce cancer risks, normalize digestion, and are good for the immune system. Spinach is best eaten raw in salads, as cooking it makes the iron harder to absorb. If you do cook it, then sweat it down in a pan or steam it.

Heart chakra imbalances lead to chest pain, breathing problems, high blood pressure, and problems with the immune system.

Blue: Throat (Vishudda) Chakra

- Blueberries, plums, red cabbage, pickled garlic, blue corn kernels (very dark blue when dried, as the flour is made into tortillas), bluefoot mushrooms (rare and exclusive to the United States, but you can also use blewit mushrooms, which are more readily available)

- Blue sage, marjoram, valerian

Borage flowers, which taste like cucumber, can be infused for tea and are known to elevate the mood.

Because of its pH chemical acidity, red cabbage, when cooked in alkaline conditions, turns a blue color. It is the best source of antioxidants, protecting against cancer and also warding off wrinkles. Imbalances can lead to sore throat, laryngitis, stiff neck, thyroid disease, hyperactivity, and anxiety.

Indigo: Brow (Ajna) Chakra

- Purple onion, black beans, eggplant, beets, kalamata olives, raisins, currants, soy beans, figs, purple potatoes, black salsify, pomegranates, elderberries, purple pepper
- Lavender, sage, thyme

Brow chakra imbalances lead to problems in the pituitary gland, eye deficiencies, learning disabilities, and swollen glands.

Violet: Crown (Sahasrara) Chakra

- Purple sprouting broccoli, purple carrots, purple cabbage, Belgium endive, black beans, prunes, black olives, aubergines (eggplant), purple onions, hass avocados, truffles, grapes, elderberries, purple striped garlic, damsons, bilberries
- Rosemary, liquorice root, vanilla beans

Crown chakra imbalances can lead to problems with the central nervous system, brain stem, and spinal cord. Migraines and headaches, mental illness, neuralgia, epilepsy, thyroid problems, throat and ear infections, hormonal disorders, PMS, bloating, and menopausal problems are all caused by an imbalance of this chakra.

Blue, indigo, and violet foods contain lutein, zeaxanthin, fiber, and flavonoids that help us to have a healthy digestive system and reduce inflammation, acting as anticarcinogens in the digestive tract and limiting the activity of cancer cells. Lutein and zeaxanthin are carotenoids that are yellow-colored phytonutrients. As the eyes are repositories for carotenoids, with lutein and zeaxanthin concentrated in the retina and lens of the eye, they protect the eyes from developing age-related macular degenerative disease and cataracts. They also protect the cells from the damaging effects of free radicals.

Flavonoids are responsible for plant colors, and there are over six thousand different substances found in virtually all plants. Plant flavonoids have been used in Oriental medicines for centuries. Berries are a great source of flavonoids.

Flavonoids help prevent blood vessels from rupturing and protect cells from oxygen damage. They enhance vitamin C and reduce inflammation.

White: Halo Chakra

· Garlic, cauliflower, Jerusalem artichoke, parsnips, shallots, turnips, kohlrabi, mushrooms, almonds, cannellini beans, butter beans, horseradish

The so-called white halo chakra is the culmination of all the energy from the seven major chakras that manifests as the halo seen around the head of certain exalted individuals. This is not to be confused with the crown chakra; however, it does reflect the holistic health of the person.

White fruits and vegetables contain nutrients such as beta-glucans, EGCG, SDG, and lignums, which provide a powerful immune-boosting activity. They activate natural killer B and T cells, which reduce the risk of colon, breast, and prostate cancers and also reduce the risk of hormone-related cancers.

Garlic is a powerful food. It lowers cholesterol and blood-sugar levels, reducing atherosclerotic buildup (plaque) within the arterial system, reducing the risk of heart attacks and strokes, and inhibiting the development of clots. Hemophiliacs shouldn't use garlic. It targets *H. pylori*, bacteria that is associated with ulcers and stomach cancers. Eating garlic can kill the bacteria and alleviate the symptoms. Raw garlic is a potent natural antibiotic, having antifungal and antiviral properties. It contains an amino acid called alliin and can kill strains of staph that are immune to modern antibiotics. It is best to peel and chop the garlic and leave it for fifteen to twenty minutes, or longer if you can, before cooking.

Horseradish stimulates the digestive system and clears the nasal passages. It can also be made into a tincture to lessen the severity of colds, flu, and coughs.

Mushrooms contain the mineral selenium and antioxidants. Low levels of selenium have been linked to increased risk of developing a more severe flu. They contain riboflavin and niacin, which help boost the immune system. Please be warned: you should not eat mushrooms raw, as they contain hydrazines, a known carcinogen.

Almonds contain riboflavin and niacin and also B vitamins. A quarter cup of almonds contains 50 percent of the daily requirement to boost the immune system. Please also remember that peanuts, which should always be eaten at their freshest, carry aflatoxin from mold contamination, a known carcinogen.

Oysters contain high levels of zinc. Low levels of zinc are linked to male infertility, hence the "lover's food" of choice.

It is also known that a daily cup of lowfat yogurt reduces the chance of getting a cold because of the live and active cultures within it.

Water is vital and pure. It lubricates joints, hydrates the lungs, and is used in the absorption and digestion of food.

Chakra Soups

The following recipes are examples of using a good range of colorful ingredients. Most soups are made in a similar way, and if you make enough for two days, put half in the refrigerator for the next day or freeze it for another time. There are no right or wrong ways to make soups; after the basic principles, if you love a certain herb, add it, or maybe you don't like spices—then leave them out. It is important to use the freshest ingredients that you can buy and treat them properly. Do not go off and leave them to boil away for a long period, as they will lose their valuable properties.

It is important to have a blender when making soups, which can be bought at a reasonable price today (from £20 sterling, or $35); some of you may have one that attaches to a food processor. You can make your own vegetable stock if you have the time, but if you haven't, use a good vegetable stock; for example, Marigold Bouillon. And if you want to add a couple tablespoons of double cream, crème fraîche, sour cream, or yogurt at the last minute or as a garnish, please do so, as a little indulgence will not hurt anybody as long as your diet is balanced.

MULADHARA: *Tomato and Roasted Red Pepper Soup*

4 large red peppers

4 garlic cloves

2 tablespoons olive oil

1 red onion, peeled and finely chopped

6 vine tomatoes

850 ml (28 fl oz/1½ pints) vegetable stock

Fresh basil leaves

Preheat the oven to 200°C (400°F/gas mark 6).

Halve the red peppers, remove seeds and pith, and place skin-side up on a baking tray. Leave the cloves of garlic in their skins and add to the tray. Roast for 30 to 35 minutes or until the skins are blistered. Place them in a plastic bag until cool, then peel off the skin and chop the flesh.

Warm the olive oil in a pan and fry the onion until softened. Chop the tomatoes and discard the seeds, then add to the onions and cook for a further 5 minutes. Add stock. Squeeze the garlic out from the skins, add to the pan, and simmer gently for 20 minutes. For the last 5 minutes, add the basil leaves. Let the soup cool before blending it in batches. Reheat gently and serve.

Serves 4.

SVADISTHANA: *Roasted Pumpkin Soup*

1 3-lb. (1.35 kg) pumpkin

1 tablespoon groundnut oil

1 large onion, peeled and finely chopped

850 ml (28 fl oz) vegetable stock

450 ml (15 fl oz) whole milk

30 g (1 oz) butter

Nutmeg, freshly grated

Salt and pepper

Preheat oven to 240°C (475°F/gas mark 9).

Cut the pumpkin into four pieces, carefully removing the stalk first. Scoop out the seeds. Place skin-side down on a baking sheet and brush the flesh with oil .Place in the oven for 20 to 25 minutes.

Melt butter in a pan and cook the onions until they color slightly; lower the heat and fry gently for 15 minutes. Then add stock and milk and leave them on a low heat to simmer very gently.

Remove the pumpkin from the oven and cool slightly. Scoop out the flesh of the pumpkin with a knife and add to the stock.

Season with salt, pepper, and nutmeg. Simmer gently for 15 to 20 minutes.

Let the soup cool slightly, and in batches put into a blender and whizz. As an extra precaution, push through a sieve to remove any fibrous bits.

When ready to eat, simmer gently to reheat—do not boil.

Serves 6.

MANIPURA: *Shellfish Chowder*

You can make your own shellfish stock using the following ingredients. Otherwise, you can buy fresh fish stock, use a fish stock cube, or, failing that, just use water.

STOCK:

    1 shallot, sliced

    30 ml (1 fl oz) rapeseed (canola) oil

    100 g (3½ oz) button mushrooms, sliced

    500 g (1 lb 2 oz) crab and lobster shells

    1 bay leaf

    400 ml (14 fl oz) water

In a large saucepan over medium heat, cook the shallot in the oil for five minutes, or until the onion is soft but not colored. Add the mushrooms and cook for 2 minutes.

Use a rolling pin to crush the shells. Turn the heat to high, add the shells and bay leaf to the onions, and cook for 4 minutes. Add water and bring to a boil. Reduce the heat and simmer for 15 minutes.

Strain the stock through a fine sieve, pressing it down with a ladle.

CHOWDER:

> 200 ml (7 fl oz) white wine
>
> 30 g (1 oz) unsalted butter
>
> 1 onion, finely diced
>
> 2 garlic cloves, sliced
>
> 1 bay leaf
>
> 400 g (14 oz) clams, washed or soaked overnight in cold water to remove sand
>
> 400 g (14 oz) mussels, cleaned, with beards removed (discard any that don't close when tapped)
>
> 200 g (7 oz) cockles, washed
>
> 200 ml (7 fl oz) shellfish stock (as above)
>
> 10 g (¼ oz) wakame seaweed, quickly washed in cold water
>
> 100 ml (3½ fl oz) whipping cream
>
> 1 cm (½ inch) piece of ginger root, peeled and grated
>
> 3 pinches ground nutmeg
>
> 3 tablespoons chopped parsley
>
> 1 lemon, juice only

Bring the wine to a boil in a small saucepan and boil it for 30 seconds, as this will remove the alcohol taste. Set aside.

In a large saucepan over medium heat, melt the butter and cook the onion and garlic for 5 minutes until soft but not colored. Increase the heat to high and add the wine; bring to a boil and cook for 1 minute. Add the bay leaf, clams, mussels, and cockles, cover with a lid, and cook for 2 minutes, until the shellfish have opened. Discard any mussels or clams that have not opened. Also discard the bay leaf.

Drain the cooked shellfish through a colander, reserving the cooking liquid, and allow to cool for a couple of minutes. Pick out the meat from the shells and set aside.

Add the shellfish cooking liquid, shellfish stock and washed seaweed back into the pan and bring to the boil. Add cream, ginger, nutmeg, shellfish, and chopped parsley. Season with salt, pepper, and lemon juice before serving.

Serves 6.

ANAHATA: *Fennel, Pea, and Mint Soup*

600 g fennel (21 oz), washed and chopped

500 g (18 oz) frozen peas

900 ml (30 fl oz) vegetable stock

3 tablespoons fresh chopped mint

Fennel has calmative properties. Fennel seeds are used in fennel tea, which calms the intestines and is an effective diuretic.

Put the fennel, peas, and stock in a large pan, bring to a boil, then reduce the heat and simmer for 20 minutes or until the fennel is tender. Add the chopped mint and simmer for a further minute. Remove a few cupfuls and set aside; allow to cool slightly, then blend in batches until smooth (keep some soup from being blended, as it will add a little texture). Add all ingredients together, reheat, and season to taste.

Serves 4.

VISHUDDA: *Bluefoot or Blewit Mushroom Soup with Pickled Garlic and Blue Cheese*

3 pints water

50 g (2 oz) dried porcini mushrooms

150 g (5 oz) butter, divided

8 shallots, finely chopped

5 fat cloves of garlic, peeled and finely chopped

900 g (2 lb) fresh bluefoot or blewit mushrooms, chopped into 1 cm pieces

4 teaspoons fresh thyme, chopped

½ teaspoon nutmeg

300 ml (10 fl oz) vegetable stock

300 ml (10 fl oz) milk

Put 3 pints of water over the porcini mushrooms, stir, and leave for 30 minutes. After 30 minutes are up, drain the porcini mushrooms over a large bowl, squeezing them out with a paper towel. Reserve the liquid.

In a large saucepan, melt 4 ounces of the butter and gently cook the shallots and garlic until soft and translucent, about 6 minutes.

Chop the porcinis into small pieces and add the other mushrooms to the shallots and garlic. Add the thyme, nutmeg, and remaining 1 oz of the butter, and carry on cooking everything for 5 minutes.

Pour in the reserved liquid and the milk, and bring to a gentle simmer for about 30 minutes without a lid, stirring occasionally.

Remove about a third and ladle the remainder in batches in the food processor and blend until smooth.

Put all the soup back in the pan and simmer very gently for 20 minutes. At this point, you can add your favorite crumbled blue cheese and serve. For a special treat, you could add Madeira to the vegetable stock.

You can also add pickled garlic at this point.

PICKLED GARLIC:

    600 ml (20 fl oz) white wine vinegar

    1 teaspoon salt

    100 g (4 oz) sugar

    10 garlic bulbs, separated into cloves

Bring vinegar, salt, and sugar to a boil and stir until the syrup is smooth. Add the garlic, bring back to a boil, and simmer for 5 minutes. Set aside to cool. Pack into sterilized jars and pour the pickling syrup over, making sure that the cloves are covered. Seal and store. Leave for a couple of weeks, as it will improve with age.

Pickled garlic does not give you garlic breath. Acid in the vinegar neutralizes the alliinase and slowly breaks down the cloves into odorless, water-soluble compounds that circulate via the bloodstream, mostly S-allyl cysteine (SAC), the active ingredient in aged garlic. SAC lowers cholesterol, blood pressure, and sugar levels, and inhibits platelet aggregation. It also has some antitumor properties; the odorless sulphides that accumulate in the lymphatic system have the greatest anticancer properties. The longer the garlic is left, the more SAC is formed.

AJNA: *Tom Yum Soup*

TOM YUM PASTE:

  2 garlic cloves

  2 lemongrass stalks

  5 cm (2 inches) fresh ginger root

  2 small bird's-eye chilies (if you don't like it
    too hot, use red chilies)

  1 small bunch of fresh coriander, stems only,
    reserve the leaves

  2 shallots

  2.5 cm (1 inch) piece palm sugar

  55 ml (2 fl oz) olive oil

SOUP:

  400 ml (14 fl oz) coconut milk

  200 ml (7 fl oz) vegetable stock

  1 handful of bean sprouts

  1 red pepper, finely sliced

  4 spring onions

  150 g (5 oz) aubergine (eggplant), sliced and chargrilled

  200 g (7 oz) peas

  16 tiger prawns, left whole

  1 lime

For the tom yum paste, place all the ingredients into the food
processor and blend. Heat a dash of olive oil and cook the paste
for 4 to 5 minutes, stirring frequently, until the smell is aromatic.

For the soup, add the coconut milk and the stock to the paste and stir well. Bring to a boil, then reduce the heat to a simmer and cook for 10 minutes.

Place the bean sprouts, peppers, and onions equally into the bottom of four serving bowls.

Stir the aubergine and peas into the soup and warm, then add the prawns and simmer until pink and cooked through.

Serve with a squeeze of lime and garnish with the coriander leaves.

Serves 4.

SAHASRARA: *Borscht with Horseradish Cream*

Although a lot of people do not like beetroot, and it is an acquired taste, the taste does grow on you if you persevere. I have loved beetroot since I was a little girl, but when I met my husband he hated it. By slowly introducing it into his diet, he now loves it, and, more importantly, because of the nitrates in the content of beetroot, it strengthens the cardiovascular muscles and helps lower blood pressure. It's also encouraging to see it in the most exclusive fine-dining restaurants, as it is used for its brilliant color, taste, and health properties.

> 1 kg (2¼ lb) beetroot, scrubbed, stalks removed
>
> 450 g (1 lb) carrots
>
> 8 shallots
>
> 2 garlic cloves, roughly chopped
>
> 1 celery stalk, chopped
>
> 1 bay leaf
>
> 500 ml (16 fl oz) vegetable stock

Peel and chop all the vegetables and place in a large pan with the bay leaf. Cover with stock and bring to a rapid boil, then reduce the heat to a simmer for about 40 minutes or until the vegetables are tender.

Remove the bay leaf and cool slightly before liquidizing the soup in batches until smooth. Pass through a medium sieve until smooth, and season to taste.

Serve with some horseradish cream. Serves 4.

HORSERADISH CREAM:
> 225 ml (8 fl oz) of crème fraîche, sour cream, or cream
> (whichever you prefer)
>
> 3 tablespoons freshly grated horseradish

If using cream, beat it first so it has a thickened consistency. Mix whatever cream you are using with the horseradish. Keep in the fridge for 2 days.

HALO: *Ajo Blanco, or Chilled Almond Soup*

200 g (7 oz) unblanched almonds

200 ml (7 fl oz) Spanish olive oil

4 cloves of garlic, peeled and left for
   at least 20 minutes before using

1 tablespoon sherry vinegar

1 teaspoon salt

350 ml (12 fl oz) cold water

To serve: 8 ice cubes and 110 g (4 oz) black
   and green grapes, deseeded and halved

First, blanch the almonds. Place them in a bowl and cover with boiling water. Leave them for 4 to 5 minutes, then drain them and squeeze them out of their skins.

Put them in a blender and pour in the olive oil so they are just covered. Add the peeled garlic, vinegar, and salt, and liquidize until everything is smooth. While the motor is still running, add the water slowly.

Pour into a bowl, cover, and keep in the refrigerator until ready to use. This can be up to three days, as it improves with age, so it would make a great summer dinner party starter.

Just before serving, stir in the ice cubes, ladle into chilled bowls, and garnish with grapes.

Serves 4.

Main Courses

Here, many beneficial foods are combined for your optimal health and energy. There are many other recipes that can use combining foods from the different chakras to maximum benefit for your well-being, and it is up to you to experiment. I am sure that you can look at the different-colored foods relating to the chakras and create your own wonderful dishes—and, more importantly, take charge of your own health and boost your energy levels.

Sea Bass with Quinoa Rice Pilau, Roasted Tomatoes, and Dill

4 sea bass, filleted

250 g (9 oz) cherry tomatoes, halved

9 tablespoons extra-virgin olive oil, divided

1 onion, finely sliced

3 celery stalks

Pinch of cumin seeds

3 garlic cloves, finely chopped

100 g (3½ oz) brown basmati rice

150 g (5 oz) quinoa

25 g (1 oz) dill

500 ml (16 fl oz) vegetable stock

50 g (2 oz) pine nuts, toasted

Heat the oven to 180°C (350°F/gas mark 4).

First, trim the sea bass fillets so they are all the same size, and then score the skin, cutting into the flesh slightly 5 or 6 times at about 1 cm intervals. Season with salt and pepper.

Put the cherry tomatoes on a baking sheet, drizzle with 3 tablespoons olive oil, and season with salt and pepper. Roast for 15 minutes, remove from the oven, and set aside.

Heat 3 tablespoons olive oil in a large pan. Add the onion, celery, cumin, and garlic. Fry on medium heat for 5 minutes or until onions are translucent. Add the rice, quinoa, dill, and stock. Cover and cook for 12 to 15 minutes or until the rice is cooked but with a slight bite to it. While this is cooking, start the fish.

Heat a frying pan until very hot and add the remaining 3 tablespoons of oil. Lay the fillets skin-side down in the pan and press down on them so they do not curl up. Reduce the heat to medium and leave the fish to cook undisturbed for 3 to 4 minutes; you will see the flesh of the fish has cooked by two-thirds and the skin is crisp and brown. Flip them over and fry the flesh for 2 minutes until cooked, while basting the skin with the oil. Leave to rest on a warm plate while you add the tomatoes and pine nuts to the quinoa rice pilau and stir gently. Serve the pilau with the sea bass fillets on top, skin-side up. Serves 4.

Pumpkin Curry with Chickpeas

2 tablespoons olive oil

3 tablespoons Thai yellow curry paste

2 onions, finely chopped

3 lemongrass stalks, crushed with the back of a knife

4 cardamom pods

1 tablespoon mustard seeds

1 kg (2.2 lb) pumpkin, peeled, quartered, seeds removed, and chopped into inch-sized pieces

250 ml (9 fl oz) vegetable stock

400 ml (14 fl oz) can coconut milk

400 g (14 fl oz) can chickpeas, drained and rinsed

2 limes—1 juiced, 1 quartered

25 g (1 oz) mint leaves

Heat the oil in a sauté pan or a heavy pan and gently fry the curry paste with the onions, lemongrass, cardamom, and mustard seeds for 3 minutes. Stir the pumpkin into the pan and coat everything in the paste, and take time to smell the fragrance of the dish. Pour in the stock and coconut milk. Add the chickpeas and bring to a simmer; cook for 10 minutes or until the pumpkin is tender. At this stage you can leave it to cool and freeze for up to one month.

To serve, add the juice of one lime. Serve the other lime's wedges alongside with torn mint leaves.

Serves 6.

SIDE DISH: *Spinach with Pine Nuts and Garlic*

1 kg (2.2 lb) leaf spinach

2 tablespoons olive oil

3 tablespoons pine nuts

3 garlic cloves, finely chopped

Wash the spinach and dry. Put into a steamer over a pan of boiling water. Cover with a lid and sweat down until wilted.

Heat the oil. Add the pine nuts and fry gently for 1 minute. Add the garlic and fry gently. Add to the spinach.

Spicy Baby Aubergine (Eggplant) Stew with Mint and Coriander

2 tablespoons olive oil

2 red onions, sliced

5 garlic cloves, crushed

2 red chilies, deseeded and sliced (wear gloves)

2 teaspoons coriander seeds, toasted
   for 2 minutes and crushed

2 teaspoons cumin seeds, toasted
   for 2 minutes and crushed

16 small aubergines (eggplants), quartered and deseeded

800 g (28 oz) passata or chopped tomatoes

1 teaspoon sugar

A handful of mint leaves and coriander leaves,
   finely chopped

Heat the oil in a heavy-based saucepan. Add the onions and garlic, but do not allow them to color. Add the chilies, coriander seeds, and cumin seeds for a couple of minutes before adding the aubergines/eggplants, onions, and spices.

Add the tomatoes and sugar, then cover gently for 30 minutes until the aubergines are tender. Add the mint and coriander, cover, and simmer for 2 minutes.

You can serve this with couscous and natural yogurt. Serves 4.

Hot Smoked Salmon, Lentil, and Pomegranate Salad

2 tablespoons extra virgin olive oil

Juice of ½ lemon

2 garlic cloves, finely chopped

2 tablespoons tarragon, finely chopped

1 teaspoon clear honey

1 small red onion, thinly sliced

400 g can puy lentils, rinsed and drained

250 g hot smoked salmon

20 g flat leaf parsley, just leaves

Seeds from 1 pomegranate

Combine the oil, lemon juice, garlic, tarragon, and honey in a large bowl and season to taste with salt and pepper. Add the red onions and puy lentils and set aside to marinate for at least 20 minutes.

Break the salmon into flakes and fold into the salad with the pomegranate seeds and the parsley.

Serves 2.

Mackerel with Griddled Vegetables

4 mackerel

2 aubergines (eggplants), cut into strips, deseeded

2 courgettes (zucchini), cut lengthwise into strips

2 red peppers, deseeded and quartered

2 large tomatoes, quartered

1 lime, juiced

Always buy whole mackerel and have it filleted. Oil-rich fish is an excellent source of fatty acids, which are essential for brain development and reducing the risk of strokes. If you can, buy line-caught fish.

Rub the mackerel with olive oil and a little salt. Put under a hot grill for 4 minutes until the flesh is opaque.

Cover the vegetables with olive oil and griddle or grill for 2 minutes on each side until tender.

Serve with the mackerel and drizzle with lime juice. Serves 4.

Tuna with Red Onion, Grape, and Raisin Confit

4 tuna steaks

2 tablespoons olive oil

CONFIT:

1 red onion, chopped

225 g (8 oz) black grapes, halved and deseeded

110 g (4 oz) raisins

350 ml (12 fl oz) red wine

55 ml (2 fl oz) red wine vinegar

1 teaspoon dark brown sugar

First, start with the confit; you can make this the day before if you wish. Put all the ingredients into a pan and bring everything up to a very gentle simmer, stirring occasionally. Let it simmer in this way without a lid for about an hour, until it resembles a sticky glaze.

When you are ready to cook the tuna, heat the oil in a heavy-based pan on medium to high heat for about 8 minutes, then put the tuna in for 2 minutes each side. Obviously some people will like them cooked a little more.

Serve with confit and a peppery salad of red baby leaves, rocket, and mizuna. Serves 4.

Tofu, Sichuan Kale, and Cashew Nuts with Stir-Fried Pak Choi (Bok Choy)

Tofu (soya/soy bean curd) is high in calcium and vitamin E and low in saturated fats. It is also high in protein and other minerals and cholesterol free. There are two main kinds of tofu; they both have different consistencies, the softer silken and the regular. Silken tofu is kept in aseptic boxes that do not require refrigeration. It is made from soybeans, water, and a coagulant incorporating calcium and magnesium in a process that is similar to making cheese. Make sure that it is fresh—you can tell this as fresh tofu has virtually no smell.

7 tablespoons olive oil, divided

110 g (4 oz) cashew nuts

½ red chili, deseeded and finely chopped (wear gloves!)

1 teaspoon Sichuan peppercorns

1 tsp chili flakes

4 shallots, finely chopped

3 teaspoons freshly chopped ginger

3 garlic cloves, finely chopped

250 g (9 oz) tofu, cut into cubes

250 g (9 oz) kale

150 g (5 oz) purple sprouting broccoli

SAUCE:

3 tablespoons soy sauce

3 tablespoons rice wine vinegar

1 tablespoon caster sugar

90 ml (3 fl oz) cold water

1 tablespoon corn flour (cornstarch) mixed to a smooth
  paste with 2 tablespoons water

STIR FRY:

2 tablespoons extra virgin olive oil

1 red chili, finely chopped

1 green chili, finely chopped

2 tablespoons freshly grated ginger

6 pak choi (bok choy), using the outer leaves only

Place 5 tablespoons olive oil in a heavy-based frying pan on medium heat and add the cashew nuts, stirring until they are golden brown. Remove with a slotted spoon and put onto kitchen paper or paper towels to drain.

In a pestle, grind the chili flakes and Sichuan peppercorns to a fine powder.

Heat the remaining oil in a wok until it is smoking, add the shallots, ginger, and garlic, and stir-fry for 2 minutes. Add the chili, ground chili flakes, and Sichuan peppercorns and continue for another minute.

Add the tofu pieces and stir-fry until pale brown, then add the kale and the purple sprouting broccoli.

In a bowl, whisk the soy sauce, rice wine vinegar, and caster sugar until combined. Add the mixture to the wok and coat the tofu and vegetables with it.

Add the water to the wok and bring it to a simmer. Cook for 3 minutes until the kale and broccoli are just tender.

Add the corn flour paste, stir well, and cook for 2 minutes or until the sauce is thickened. Add the cashew nuts and stir well. Keep warm.

For the stir fry, heat 2 tablespoons oil in a separate wok or frying pan on high heat. When the oil is smoking, add the ginger and chilies and stir-fry for 2 minutes. Add the pak choi (bok choy) leaves and continue to fry for 2 minutes or until just wilted.

Serve the tofu, kale, and cashew nuts with the pak choi (bok choy) alongside. Serves 4.

Walnut and Lentil Burgers

2 tablespoons extra virgin olive oil

1 small carrot, finely chopped

1 celery stick, chopped

100 g (3½ oz) walnuts, finely chopped

100 g (3½ oz) button mushrooms

1 teaspoon thyme, chopped

1 tablespoon parsley, chopped finely

½ teaspoon salt

1 teaspoon ground black pepper

200 g (7 oz or 2 cups) cooked brown rice

400 g can of cooked lentils, rinsed to remove the sodium

1 egg

Heat the olive oil in a frying pan. Add the carrots, celery, walnuts, mushrooms, thyme, parsley, salt and pepper and fry gently for about five minutes until softened. Transfer to a bowl.

In a food processor, purée 1 cup of rice, lentils, and egg until smooth. Transfer to the vegetable bowl, add the remaining cup of rice, and stir to combine.

Mix into 8 2- to 3-inch diameter burgers and cook until crisp, about 10 minutes. Serves 4.

Hass Avocado and Mango Salsa

4 fully ripened Mexican hass avocados, diced

2 tablespoons lime juice

4 plum tomatoes, diced

2 tablespoons white wine vinegar

2 small mangoes, peeled and chopped

1 jalapeño pepper, deseeded and finely chopped

115 g (4 oz) chopped cilantro

3 garlic cloves, minced

½ red onion, chopped finely

2 tablespoons olive oil

Salt and pepper

Toss together and serve on its own or with salmon.

Blueberry, Tofu, and Banana Smoothie

Pack of silken tofu

1 banana

1 cup unsweetened soy milk

½ cup blueberries

1 teaspoon honey

3 ice cubes

Drain the silken tofu to remove the excess water. Peel and slice the banana, place on a plate, and freeze for 15 minutes.

Blend the banana, tofu, and soy milk for 30 seconds. Add the blueberries, honey, and ice cubes and blend for a further 30 seconds. Serves 1.

Blueberry Chutney

This is particularly good with swordfish, but it is also very good with goat cheese and most hot or cold meats, including game.

1 tablespoon olive oil

2 shallots, sliced thinly

2 punnets (2 cups) blueberries

1 tablespoon sugar

Pinch of ground cinnamon

Pinch of ground cloves

Pinch of allspice

2 tablespoons cider vinegar

Sauté the shallots in the olive oil; do not let them brown. Add the blueberries, sugar, and spices, and shake the pan to combine.

Add the cider vinegar and cook over medium heat for 3–4 minutes or until the sauce has thickened.

Spoon into sterilized jars and keep in a cool place for up to 4 weeks.

Beetroot Purée

This is a beautifully colored purée that can be added to fish, meat, tofu, or even ice cream!

> 600 g (38 oz) raw beetroot
>
> 4 cloves garlic, peeled
>
> 100 g (3½ oz) shelled walnuts
>
> ½ teaspoon each salt and pepper
>
> 20 g (¾ oz) coriander leaves (cilantro)
>
> 10 g (½ oz) flat-leaf parsley
>
> ½ teaspoon ground coriander
>
> 4 teaspoons red wine vinegar

Preheat the oven to 220°C (425°F/gas mark 7).

Wrap the beetroots loosely in foil so the air can circulate but seal them tightly so that the steam circulates. Roast for about 2 hours but check after an hour by piercing with a knife. Cool completely.

Put the garlic in the food processor and blitz until finely minced. Add the walnuts, salt, and pepper, and process again.

Wearing rubber gloves, peel and chop the beetroot. Add it to the food processor along with the herbs and ground coriander and process until you have a paste.

Add the red wine vinegar and pulse again. Taste the purée, as the beetroot can be a little sweet. If it is too sweet for your taste, just add more red wine vinegar.

Cover and leave to marinate for a few hours. Serves 8 as an accompaniment.

Desserts

Combining many of the fruits that we have mentioned here is the best way to eat these fruits healthily. You can add lowfat crème fraîche, yogurt, or cream.

Fruit Kebabs with Mango and Yogurt Sauce

I small pineapple, peeled, cored, and cubed

2 kiwi fruit, peeled and cubed

150 g (5 oz) strawberries, hulled and cut lengthwise

I mango, peeled and cubed

SAUCE:

    120 ml (4 fl oz) fresh mango purée (made by puréeing
      one mango)

    120 ml (4 fl oz) thick plain natural yogurt

    I teaspoon caster sugar

    Few drops of vanilla extract

    I tablespoon finely shredded mint leaves
      plus I sprig to decorate

To make the sauce, blend the mango purée, yogurt, sugar, and vanilla. Stir in shredded mint. Cover the sauce with cling film and chill.

Thread the fruits, alternating them, onto wooden skewers.

Transfer the dip to an attractive bowl; decorate it with the mint sprig and surround with the kebabs. Obviously you can vary this dish with your favorite fruits. Serves 4.

Conclusion

The nadi technique considers the whole person; regardless of what you are endeavoring to achieve from the program, a healthy, well-balanced diet should be an integral part of this. Apart from being appetizing and healthy, the foods from the previous chapter help in the regulation of energy and the polarization of the chakra system, encouraging you to be more focused in your endeavors.

As mentioned, it is not necessary to use all the techniques in the program, as each method is a complete technique in itself. Once you have accustomed yourself to the nadi technique and fully understand the way it works, you should then formulate your own working program to be used whenever you feel a need.

I wish you well in your endeavors and sincerely hope that you will derive a great deal of benefit from the nadi technique.

Works Cited

Babbitt, Edwin D, *Principles of Light and Color*. A look at the healing powers of color.

Benson, Herbert, *Science Daily Magazine* and *New Thought Directory* (2000). The effects of meditation on the brain.

Croxon Byerly, Paula, *Dictionary of Mind, Body and Spirit*. Details the work of Semyon and Valentina's research with their aura camera.

Copen, Bruce, *Magic of the Aura*. Russian research into bioplasma bodies and human bioluminescence, a look at Walter Kilner's work with the development of his aura screens.

Leadbeater, C. W., *The Etheric Body*. Integration of the cells into a whole.

Luders, Eileen, "Long-term effects of meditation on the brain," *NeuroImage Magazine* (2000, repr. 2012). Observed differences in brain cells of meditators.

Lysebeth, Andre Van, *Pranayama*. Assessing chakra deficiency through a person's gait.

Luftermier, Hans, *Psychology of Sleep* (Gultner Press, 1954). Study in consciousness.

Mesmer, Friedrich Anton, in Theresa Cheung's *Element Encyclopedia of the Psychic World* (Harper Element, 2006). How the innovator of mesmerism used magnetic energy to heal sickness.

Metzner, Ralph, *Map of Consciousness*. Use and effects of hallucinogenic compounds to promote higher states of consciousness.

Powel, Arthur E., *The Etheric Double*. A detailed look at the etheric body.

Ramacharaka, Yogi, *Fourteen Lessons in Yogi Philosophy and Oriental Occultism*. A look at the seven bodies, referred to as 7 principles in yoga.

———, *Raja Yoga* (Fowler, 1915, repr. 2012). Thought waves and vibrations.

Tutinsky, Ivan, in Ramacharaka's *Advanced Course in Yogi Philosophy*. Research into the functioning of the pineal gland in paranormal experience.

Recommended Reading

Babbitt, Edwin D. *Principles of Light and Color*. Kessinger, 2010.

Baker, Douglas. *The Human Aura*. Baker Publications, 1975, repr. 2000.

———. *Super Consciousness Through Meditation*. Thorsons, 1975; Baker Publications, 2000.

Besant, Annie. *The Etheric Double*. Kessinger, 2006.

———. *Thought Power*. Kessinger, 1899, repr. 2000.

Blades, Dudley. *Healing Hands*. Thorsons, 1975.

Copen, Bruce. *Magic of the Aura*. Academic Publications, 1975.

Croxon, Paula Byerly. *The Piatkus Dictionary of Mind, Body and Spirit*. Piatkus Books, 2003.

Devi, Indra. *Forever Young, Forever Healthy*. Thorsons, 1956, repr. 1980.

Jinarajadasa, C. *First Principles of Theosophy*. Theosophical Publications, 1890, repr. 2010.

Kilner, Walter. *The Human Aura*. Kessinger, 2003.

Leadbeater, C. W. *The Chakras*. Theosophical Publications, 1922, repr. 2012.

———. *The Etheric Body*. Theosophical Society, 1890, repr. 2012.

McTaggart, Lynne. *The Field*. Harper, 2007.

Metzner, Ralph. *Map of Consciousness*. World Publications, 1976.

Motoyama, Hiroshi. *Theories of the Chakras Bridge to Higher Consciousness.* Quest Books, 1988.

Powel, Arthur E. *The Etheric Double.* Theosophical, 2007.

Ramacharaka, Yogi. *Advanced Course in Yogi Philosophy.* Book Jungle, 2008.

———. *The Fourteen Lessons in Yogi Philosophy and Oriental Occultism.* Fowler, 1903, repr. 2005, 2012.

———. *Gnani Yoga.* Fowler, 1903, repr. 2012.

———. *Water Therapy.* Fowler, 1903, repr. 2012.

Roberts, Billy. *The Magic of the Aura.* Apex Publications, 2008.

———. *Psychology of a Medium.* O-Books, 2012.

———. *So You Want To Be a Healer.* Watkins, 2011.

———. *A Wag's As Good As a Smile.* 6th Books, 2012.

Trattler, Ross. *Better Health Through Natural Healing.* Thorsons, 1980.

van Lysebeth, Andre. *Pranayama.* Harmony Publications, 1980.

Index

GET MORE AT LLEWELLYN.COM

Visit us online to browse hundreds of our books and decks, plus sign up to receive our e-newsletters and exclusive online offers.

- Free tarot readings • Spell-a-Day • Moon phases
- Recipes, spells, and tips • Blogs • Encyclopedia
- Author interviews, articles, and upcoming events

GET SOCIAL WITH LLEWELLYN

Find us on Facebook

www.Facebook.com/LlewellynBooks

Follow us on

www.Twitter.com/Llewellynbooks

GET BOOKS AT LLEWELLYN

LLEWELLYN ORDERING INFORMATION

 Order online: Visit our website at www.llewellyn.com to select your books and place an order on our secure server.

 Order by phone:
- Call toll free within the U.S. at 1-877-NEW-WRLD (1-877-639-9753)
- Call toll free within Canada at 1-866-NEW-WRLD (1-866-639-9753)
- We accept VISA, MasterCard, and American Express

 Order by mail:
Send the full price of your order (MN residents add 6.875% sales tax) in U.S. funds, plus postage and handling to: Llewellyn Worldwide, 2143 Wooddale Drive Woodbury, MN 55125-2989

POSTAGE AND HANDLING

STANDARD (U.S. & Canada):
(Please allow 12 business days)
$25.00 and under, add $4.00.
$25.01 and over, FREE SHIPPING.

INTERNATIONAL ORDERS (airmail only):
$16.00 for one book, plus $3.00 for each additional book.

Visit us online for more shipping options. Prices subject to change.

FREE CATALOG!

To order, call
1-877-NEW-WRLD
ext. 8236
or visit our website

To order, call 1-877-NEW-WRLD

Prices subject to change without notice

The Complete Book of Chakra Healing
Activate the Transformative Power
of Your Energy Centers
Cyndi Dale

When first published in 1996 as *New Chakra Healing*, Cyndi Dale's guide to the chakras established a new standard for healers, intuitives, and energy workers worldwide. This groundbreaking book quickly became a bestseller. It expanded the seven-chakra system to thirty-two chakras, explained spiritual points available for dynamic change, and outlined the energetic system so anyone could use it for health, prosperity, and happiness.

Presented here for the first time is the updated and expanded edition, now titled *The Complete Book of Chakra Healing*. With nearly 150 more pages than the original book, this groundbreaking edition is poised to become the next classic guide to the chakras. This volume presents a wealth of valuable new material:

- the latest scientific research explaining the subtle energy system and how it creates the physical world

- depiction of the negative influences that cause disease, as well as ways to deal with them

- explanations of two dozen energy bodies plus the meridians and their uses for healing and manifesting

978-0-7387-1502-5

$24.95, 7½ x 9⅛, 456 pp.

To order, call 1-877-NEW-WRLD

Prices subject to change without notice

Mother Nature's Herbal
A Complete Guide for Experiencing the Beauty, Knowledge, and Synergy of Everything that Grows

Judith Griffin, Ph.D.

Due to overwhelming demand since its debut ten years ago, this beloved guide to the herbal wisdom of Mother Nature is back! With ancient folklore, simple instructions for growing an herb garden, and recipes from around the world, *Mother Nature's Herbal* is hands-down the most unique, thoughtful, and comprehensive guide to growing and preparing herbs.

Divided into useful sections and graced with charming illustrations, this book is the perfect addition to any budding herbalist's kitchen counter. Part one presents a rich tapestry of centuries-old customs, recipes, and mythology from various cultures, including Native American, South American, Asian, Mediterranean, medieval, colonial, and more.

Part two explains how to grow and use your own organic herbs. Make them thrive with tips on tending the soil, guarding against pests, and keeping your plants healthy. Once you've harvested your herbs, experiment with an assortment of recipes for foods, teas, tonics, ointments, and medicines. Explore the magical benefits of herbs, and enjoy invigorated health and a rejuvenated spirit!

978-0-7387-1256-7

$24.95, 7½ x 9⅛, 432 pp.

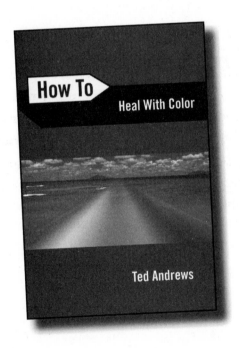

How To

Heal With Color

Ted Andrews

To order, call 1-877-NEW-WRLD

Prices subject to change without notice

ORDER AT LLEWELLYN.COM 24 HOURS A DAY, 7 DAYS A WEEK!

How to Heal with Color

Ted Andrews

Color vibrations can interact with the human energy system to stabilize physical, emotional, mental, and spiritual conditions. This book helps you develop psychic sensitivity to color vibrations, gives beneficial colors for over fifty conditions, and teaches you to balance the chakras, construct a healing mandala, rejuvenate your health, and determine what colors you need through dowsing and muscle testing.

978-0-7387-0811-9

$9.95, 5³/₁₆ x 7⁵/₈, 192 pp.

To order, call 1-877-NEW-WRLD

Prices subject to change without notice

ORDER AT LLEWELLYN.COM 24 HOURS A DAY, 7 DAYS A WEEK!

The Awakened Aura
Experiencing the Evolution of Your Energy Body
Kala Ambrose

Humanity is entering a new era—we are evolving into super-powered beings of light. Our auric and etheric bodies are experiencing a transformational shift as new crystalline structures form within and around our auras. Kala Ambrose, a powerful wisdom teacher, intuitive, and oracle, teaches how to connect with your rapidly changing energy body to expand your awareness and capabilities on the physical, mental, emotional, and spiritual levels.

This book contains a wealth of practical exercises, diagrams, and instructions. Learn how to interpret and work with the auras of others, sense energy in animals, and sense and balance the energy in buildings and natural locations. Discover how energy cords attach in relationships, how to access the akashic records through the auric layers, how to use elemental energy to enhance your auric field, and much more.

978-0-7387-2759-2
$14.95, 6 x 9, 240 pp.

To order, call 1-877-NEW-WRLD

Prices subject to change without notice

ORDER AT LLEWELLYN.COM 24 HOURS A DAY, 7 DAYS A WEEK!

Chakra Awakening
Transform Your Reality Using Crystals, Color,
Aromatherapy & the Power of Positive Thought

Margaret Ann Lembo

Bring balance, prosperity, joy, and overall wellness to your life. Use gemstones and crystals to tap into the amazing energy within you—the chakras.

This in-depth and practical guide demonstrates how to activate and balance the seven main chakras—energy centers that influence everything from migraines and fertility to communication and intuition. Perform simple techniques with gems, crystals, and other powerful tools to manifest any goal and create positive change in your physical, emotional, and spiritual wellbeing.

Chakra Awakening also features color photos and exercises for clearing negative energy, dispelling outdated belief systems, and identifying areas in your life that may be out of balance.

978-0-7387-1485-1
$19.95, 6 x 9, 264 pp.

To Write to the Author

If you wish to contact the author or would like more information about this book, please write to the author in care of Llewellyn Worldwide and we will forward your request. Both the author and the publisher appreciate hearing from you and learning of your enjoyment of this book and how it has helped you. Llewellyn Worldwide cannot guarantee that every letter written to the author can be answered, but all will be forwarded. Please write to:

Billy Roberts
ᶜ/₀ Llewellyn Worldwide
2143 Wooddale Drive
Woodbury, MN 55125-2989
Please enclose a self-addressed stamped envelope for reply
or $1.00 to cover costs. If outside the USA, enclose
an international postal reply coupon.

Many of Llewellyn's authors have websites with additional information and resources. For more information, please visit our website:

WWW.LLEWELLYN.COM